# Broke Hungry & Happy

# The Life of Dangerous Dave Norell

By Rae Ann Norell

**Broke Hungry and Happy**

Cover Design, Tara Mayberry
Cover Photo, Rapid Magazine Cover, Spring 2004.
Photo by Braden Fandrich

Borderline Publishing LLC
406 S 3rd Street
Boise ID 83702
www.borderlinepublishing.com

Library of Congress Control Number: 2011938621

ISBN 978-1936408801 (Paperback)
ISBN 978-1936408405 (eBook)

I. Title

2011

This novel is a work of nonfiction. Most names and incidents are used with permission granted to the author, others have been changed and characteristics related to them have been changed.

Printed in the United States of America on post-consumer recycled paper

# With love to:

| | |
|---|---|
| My son | David Michael Norell |
| My daughter | Amy Hergert |
| My son-in-law | Travis Hergert |
| David's father | Mike Norell |

My grandchildren:

Anna Claire
Josef David
Bennett Raymond
and

**the many family and friends David loved and who loved him.**

# TRIBUTE TO MY FRIEND, DAVID

## May 22, 1979- April 24, 2004

My mind was aghast as I arose today to find myself at a loss.
How do I pay tribute? I really don't know.

The ocean of mirrored glass beneath my winged-carrier
To the community of friends paying respect to a soul.

What a life! Twenty-four and ripe,
Eager experiences like memories played it with gold.

Living for yourself. Some said selfish, myself included.
Was I misdirected? Absolutely!

My respect is deep, I looked up, idolized---
And suddenly you were gone.

Do you know I felt this way? Loved you?
And how I couldn't believe you'd slipped away?

Falling and crashing off of rocks, under trees.
Multi-day Sierra trips, pilgrimage to BC.

For all you've done and been called,
"Dangerous Dave" was no joke.

With enough motivation, strength and drive,
I will pray for your Love with
The number of days I'm alive.

Dan Menten
April 29, 2004

# Acknowledgments

Many of David's friends shared personal stories which I've incorporated into the book. In particular, I thank Dan Menten, Andrew West, Tyler Smith, Graham Wright, Joe Carberry, Chad Crabtree, Scott Feindell, Braden Fandrich, Corey Boux, Corey Volt, Kelli Jeffress, Leland Davis, Jay Moffatt, Jordan Dew, Dustin Urizar, and Eric Link. I appreciate Tao Berman and Nikki Kelly previewing the book and offering their comments for the back cover. There are many others who offered insights as well and they are all deeply appreciated.

I would like to thank Angela Meuser for editing the book and for the creative suggestions she gave. Linda Paul, my writing consultant, deserves special thanks for the many hours she devoted to helping me. I'm grateful to Borderline Publishing for their guidance and for helping me get the book to print. Kudos to Tara Mayberry, a gifted graphic artist, for bringing the cover of my book to life.

I'm so grateful to my writing group, Boise Word Spinners, for listening to David's story and for their valuable insight and friendship as I finished the book. They helped me realize the goal I've had for seven years: completion of this book. I thank them for their belief in me.

I'm thankful to David for the journals, articles, and video footage he left. Not only were these invaluable in my effort to write about his life, but most importantly they keep his memory vivid in my mind.

I thank my daughter for putting up with me while I worked on this project. Her encouragement has been a blessing.

# Preface

When my son David died on April 24, 2004, I was devastated. Shortly after the whirlwind first week of preparations for the memorial, and family and friends gathering to support and console us, I had what many bereaved parents experience, a fear that I would forget the details of David's life. Being a bit of a "Type A" personality, about three weeks after he passed, I typed a ten-page outline of his life. I was still working full time and playing in the Boise Philharmonic, but I vowed that I would write a book about David's life when I retired.

Better than my outline and memories, I was most fortunate that David left us with over 50 hours of raw footage depicting his life and adventures, as well as numerous articles and writings, both published and unpublished. From these I have drawn inspiration and discovered details that enrich this story greatly. He also had a brief "bio" of his life on his computer that outlined the main events, kayak trips, and people he met from age 18-24. In a sense, David is the "ghost writer" for this book, and as such I chose to put Part I in first person from David's viewpoint. After his death in the Prologue and Part II, the narrative is in my own voice.

I retired in September of 2009. During periods of insomnia I planned the first two chapters as well as the essence of the rest of the book. Then I'd crawl out of bed and type my ideas. In November 2009 I had surgery. After being sedated I was informed the doctor was behind schedule and my surgery would be delayed by one hour. I asked the nurse to hand me a tiny spiral notebook and a pencil from my purse, and proceeded to hand write chapters one and two of the book. (Drugs help, right?) I began to type the book as soon as I recovered from the surgery.

Over the years David's good friends have been kind enough to stay in touch with me. With the advent of social networking it has become easier to find them and continue the connection. They have been a blessing to me. These friends are a big part of this story;

without them David would not have had the adventures he had, in the US, Canada and all over the world.

I lacked one thing--- a thorough understanding of the kayaking terminology and details of how these young men and women scouted, set up safety, portaged, decided on a line to follow, etc. I was not a kayaker, I was just a "Kayak Mom." I am thankful to Dan Menten, Andrew West, Graham Wright and other close friends of David's for helping me with the terminology and also filling me in on their adventures.

Writing this book has been a journey of discovery and re-discovery for me, and I've so enjoyed the project. It has brought laughter and tears. I hope all of you enjoy the book and whether you knew David or not, that you gain inspiration from his brief life, and his philosophy of living life to the fullest, and most importantly, doing what you love to do!

# Table of Contents

# PART II

**Chapter 41**

# Prologue

### Tragedy Strikes
### April 24, 2004

I was excited to finish the morning rehearsal with the Boise Philharmonic so I could finish packing for my two week tour of China. That night the Philharmonic would be playing the final concert of the season, so I would be getting to bed late. The next morning I was to meet a group of fellow travelers at the airport at 11 a.m.

It seemed like the last minute details of packing for an overseas trip always took the longest. Got my novel? Check. Got my camera? Check. Got my passport, visa, and itinerary? Check. Got my tip money? Check. Got my new Mandarin dictionary? Check. I was very organized, traveled a lot, and knew how to make a good packing list.

At 3:30 p.m. the phone rang. Thinking it might be my son David calling to tell me how he had done in the triathlon he had competed in that morning, I answered the phone. "Hello?"

"Is this David Norell's mother?" a man asked.

"Yes?" I replied, a bit curious.

"I'm Joe Carberry. I organized the race that your son was in today."

"Yes?" I was slightly worried now.

"Your son had a problem."

"What happened?" I asked anxiously. I was pretty worried now, thinking perhaps he broke his arm or leg and was in the hospital. The thought flashed through my mind that if David had broken his arm or some such, I might not be able to go to China the next day. Then I had a chilling thought that he had trouble with his heart and was in the hospital.

By this time my boyfriend Howard noticed my concerned tone and approached me. I motioned for him to come closer.

Joe said, "He's not with us."

"What do you mean?" I asked. My pulse must have shot up to 100 beats per minute, but at the same time, my heart stood still.

"He didn't make it," Joe said.

"What do you mean?" I exclaimed, now in a panic, not able to imagine the worst, but fearing I knew exactly what Joe was having such a difficult time saying. I had to be certain and make him say it.

The only thing I don't remember from this tragic conversation that irrevocably changed my life forever, was what Joe finally had to say to get me to believe and understand. He must have said, "He died," or, "He passed on." At which point I countered with, "Is this a *joke?*!"

Joe said, "No, I'm so sorry." I sank to the floor and slid the phone across the carpet to Howard. Somehow I had the presence of mind to say to Howard, "Get his phone number and find out what happened," before I slammed my bedroom door, and stomped around the room in a half-crouch yelling "No! No! No!" just like I had seen portrayed in movies when something like this happened to other people. But it was never supposed to happen to me.

# PART I

# Chapter 1

## Bear Creek

Adrenaline pounded through my veins, almost as loudly as the roar of the 70-foot, two-tiered waterfall in front of me. I visualized my line. Splashing water on my face a couple of times, I positioned my yellow Pyranha kayak, put the paddle-blade in the water and pushed off the brink. Punching the entrance hole placed me right where I wanted to be----coming off the lip. When I connected with the shelf my boat skipped forward, defying the laws of physics.[1]

I landed the first 25 –foot drop flat, before flailing off the forty-five like a feather. [2] Landing tail first after the second drop the bow of my boat came down so hard that I slammed into the top of my kayak, barely registering the pain. I was ecstatic. I tapped the top of my yellow helmet two times, signifying to my friends on the bank of the river, that I was ok. My friend Joe yelled, "Yea Dave! Yea Dave!"

It was June 2, 2003 and Dan Menten, Joe Carberry, Chad Randol, Korey Dausz and I left Boise at 6:00 that morning. Bear Creek runs into Wildhorse River near Cambridge, Idaho. We ran part of the river with smaller drops first and some great bouldery-creeking. Then we came upon this massive drop that I knew I just had to attempt. During scouting we all agreed there was no telling what the transition would do. I thought I could get a stroke and make the move, so I was stoked to run it. The others opted not to. Joe set up the video camera from the top and Dan took the footage from below. Everybody made the difficult portage above a rocky landing, passing their boats as a team.

It was an awesome, bright, sunny day, and I was happy to be alive, doing my favorite thing in life. But my story starts 24 years earlier...

# Chapter 2

## A Kayaker is Born

Mom was so ready for me to arrive. At the time she was interim concertmaster of the Boise Philharmonic. She later told me that three weeks before I was born she had to "waddle" to the stage to perform in Boise and the next night in Twin Falls--- a two-hour drive from Boise. They played Beethoven's Ninth Symphony, which according to violinists, is a backbreaking long piece, even if you aren't nine months pregnant.

Tired of being cooped up for the last nine months, I arrived kicking my way into this world on Tuesday May 22, 1979, 12:40 a.m. I weighed in at a whopping seven pounds, fourteen ounces. Mom tells me she first felt labor pains at 10:30 p.m., just two hours before I made my appearance. I had kicked her so hard it broke her waters. Almost immediately the labor pains were five minutes apart. Maybe I knew I had a lot of living and excitement waiting for me, so I didn't want to waste another moment trapped in the womb.

My sister Amy, three and one half years older, looked at me in the hospital nursery room, swaddled in a blue blanket, pointed to the baby next to me, wrapped in a pink blanket, and said, "I want that one." I guess she thought it was a baby store. I was told that the day my parents brought me home, Mom was changing my diaper while Amy looked on with a serious expression on her face. She pointed at me and said, "Oh! He has one of *those*!" Thus she established right away I was a boy---her little brother. In a few days my grandparents Calvin and Evangeline Bromfield from Denver came to spend a week with our little family.

When I was three weeks old, Mom took me for my well baby checkup. My pediatrician detected a heart murmur. To assuage Mom's anxiety he said, "It's probably nothing, but we better get this checked out, just in case he has some condition that needs to be corrected by surgery." He sent us downtown for a chest x-ray. Mom relates I cried loudly in protest when they strapped me to a board. The pediatric cardiologist deemed my heart murmur benign meaning "harmless." He told Mom they were quite common and nothing to worry about. However to be on the safe side, I was to have an EKG every three years, which my mother attended to religiously. All of those turned out normal.

# Chapter 3

## Childhood

Amy and I were small, only 19 or 20 pounds at 12 months, both of us fairly bald---so we looked about six or seven months old when we began walking at nine months. My parents had us around water early on. We were in "Mommy and Me" swim classes at the Y and were wading in the Boise River by 18 months old. There is video of me holding Dad's hand running towards the waves that wash up on shore at Cannon Beach, Oregon. I would pull back, hesitant to dip my toes into the ocean. I wore my first wetsuit at age seven at Cannon Beach; it was Dad's, so of course was way too big.

My grandmother Dorothy Norell, like all grandmas, liked to spoil us. She always brought candy in a little paper bag for us when she visited. I was about three when my parents pulled Grandma aside one day and asked her not to bring candy any more, just healthy snacks. Not knowing about this request, next time Grandma came over I ran eagerly to hug her and quickly take our little bag of goodies. I opened up the bag only to find bananas and raisins, and threw the fruit on the floor in a little tantrum. Grandma returned to bringing us candy after that.

I loved to scare my mom, which was an easy thing to do. One time I threw a rubber spider at her and listened to her squeal. Another time I hid in the closet and watched her practically faint when she opened the door and found me standing there staring quietly at her, not moving an inch.

We played various board games, especially in the winter. Even as a little boy I was bored with winter because I didn't like to stay inside or sit still very long. To this day Mom and Dad don't know how I managed to do so well in the game called Memory. The object is to find matching pairs of pictures. The player concentrates like crazy when the other people turn over their cards so he can try to remember where the pairs are. In between turns I appeared not to be paying attention because I was standing on my head or rolling around the floor, but I usually got a match when my turn came around again.

My parents have degrees in music and met as school music teachers. With Dad playing French Horn in the Boise Philharmonic, and Mom on violin, they hired babysitters a couple of evenings a week while they attended rehearsals. This was great fun. The sitters would clean up the messes I made, and they'd chase me if I ran around the house yelling. At that time we had a very large, two-story house, and I knew where to hide so the sitters couldn't find me. My sister tried to help them. I'd generally not mind, making it difficult for them to get me to bed. One time when my sister was seven she wrote a note to my parents that said, "David was really bad and wouldn't mind at all. I was an angel." The sitter told my parents that I wasn't *that* bad, and that Amy wasn't perfect either.

When I was about six, Mom looked out her bedroom window and saw me high up in a big tree. She shouted at me to get down immediately. Lest you think I was always brave, I did have a few phobias. I was afraid of dogs, horses, and bees. The dog fear makes perfect sense, since at age two a huge dog barked and nipped near my face. I was afraid of dogs until my parents bought me a sweet eight-week old Brittany Spaniel when I was 13. I picked Jenny out of the litter because she was the smallest one of the bunch, kind of like me. We named her "Lady Jennifer of Pomona"--- Pomona being the street we lived on. After all she was pure bred and we had to have a fancy name for her. We shortened it to Jenny.

I was in Boy Scouts from fourth through sixth grade. Dad and I worked long and hard on my little car for the pinewood derby race. Our car came in first place and I received a trophy to add to my collection of trophies for football, baseball, soccer, BMX bike racing, and later, wrestling--- all of which Mom kept after I moved out.

My parents told me I experienced night terrors. These can be pretty frightening for parents. The child having them is usually asleep with his or her eyes open, often screaming or yelling. Evidently I said the same thing every time it happened. "Make the room stop spinning, make it stop!" They took me out in the cool air, held me and tried to calm me down. Eventually I woke up. A nurse explained to Mom that it might have been related to having a fever.

A couple of times when I was at Boy Scout Camp, I'd wake up in the middle of the night screaming. The leaders came running thinking a bear had got me. I'd often have squirmed my way upside down in my sleeping bag and couldn't breathe. I struggled to wake up and get out of my bag. After that first time, they always put my tent farther away from everyone.

My parents enrolled me in all sorts of sports. Besides swimming, I was in gymnastics, BMX bike racing, karate, kick-boxing (which my mother didn't like), softball, soccer, and in fourth grade through sixth grade, football. I was also into skateboarding, skiing, and later on snowboarding.

I wasn't too attentive in baseball, especially if they put me out in the field; I did somersaults waiting for something interesting to happen until the coach yelled at me to redirect my attention. I liked to slide into the bases even when it wasn't necessary. In soccer, if the coach placed me as goalie, I tried to climb the goal net, and bounced around if nothing seemed to be happening at the moment. I wasn't goalie for long. The videos of me playing soccer show me falling down all the time; it's as if I was falling down on purpose.

I was lucky in football; since I was so small they put me in a team with boys two years younger to be more equally matched in size. Thus I was the most coordinated and fastest on the team. However by seventh grade, I would have had to be in the regular seventh grade team. I was too small so I took up wrestling instead and of course later, kayaking.

I loved to dress up in the various uniforms involved in all the sports. I practiced my karate and kick-boxing moves in my uniforms in the kitchen, with accompanying kicks and shouts, often with my face painted black or some other color. I zoomed around the house wearing camouflage or Superman outfits. I somersaulted down the hall to my bedroom from the living room more often than I walked.

When I was nine I had a couple of close calls. We lived near a very busy street and there wasn't a stoplight where I crossed to get to one of my favorite hangouts---Pojo's. One day I sideswiped a car while crossing on my bike. Fortunately it was rush hour so the traffic was stop and go. The driver wasn't too happy that I broke his side view mirror.

I only had one major injury during my childhood, which was amazing considering how active I was. One time when I was sledding near Camelback Park I hit a rock. Next thing I knew I was airborne, then I was in a ditch. Jason's mom was worried about the blood streaming down my face from a cut above my eye.

"Just take me home, I hate doctors," I said to her. She rushed me to the ER anyway. Mom got home from shopping about an hour after this incident and Amy told her, "Somebody called, and David is at the hospital. He was in a sledding accident." This was before the days of cell phones. Not having more information than that, Mom was very upset as she drove down to the hospital wondering how bad it was.

I forgot to mention one other fear I had: a fear of needles. When Mom arrived, the hospital staff told her that I had been yelling hysterically, saying, "Don't do anything until my parents get here!" They finally had to give me an injection to calm me down. When Mom saw me I was lying sedated on the gurney and I'd already received six stitches. She later told me how bad she felt that she hadn't been there from the start, but was very relieved that I hadn't damaged my eye That evening I said, "I hope I'll have a scar; I love scars."

My parents wanted Amy and me to play an instrument. Amy was quite talented and played violin from age six, as well as piano and singing. I probably inherited the "music gene" too, but I didn't want to sit still long enough to practice every day. Dad had me try baritone horn for a few weeks at age seven. He said I did quite well. Grandma Norell was upset that I wouldn't even take piano since all of her children "had to" take piano lessons.

Mom used to host recitals for her students twice a year in our home. Amy also played her violin. From age five to seven, they dressed me up in a white shirt, slacks and a little black bow tie--- I had to sing a song in the recital. I could carry a tune, so was accepted into All City Kiwanis Boys' Choir after my audition in the fourth grade, but that only lasted a year. One summer with the bribe of money from my parents, I took summer school band and played trumpet and did alright, but it just wasn't my thing. I took the money and that was the end of that--- until I played guitar for awhile in high school.

I hated doing chores although my parents didn't give me that many. When I was about seven I often pouted and stomped around saying, "I *hate* jobs!" whenever Mom or Dad reminded me to complete a chore. One thing Mom later said about me was that whenever I'd get into a temper, I'd quickly be over it and back to a good mood.

I made friends easily; because of my size I often befriended younger boys as I could be the "leader." I remember one time when I was five, I came home crying to my mom and said " Nick is moving." Mom asked why I thought that. I said, "Because there's a 'for sale' sign in his front yard." Mom walked over there later, and came back and said, "They aren't moving; that was an election sign." I couldn't read yet and thought it said "for sale."

\*\*\*

School was not my favorite thing. Almost every year my parents had to work with the teachers for a couple of weeks to help them understand my activity level, and to help me understand what I needed to do to succeed in a particular teacher's classroom. I invariably got in trouble with substitute teachers. In the first few grades I'd be walking down the aisle, arms swinging, sometimes accidentally knocking books off desks or hitting someone; yes accidentally. I couldn't sit still and often dangled precariously from the edge of the chair or fell off.

In first grade my mom got a call from the principal because I had pushed the first bike in a row of parked bicycles and they all toppled like dominoes. After being properly chastised by the principal and Mom, we drove home in a hurry because Mom had only 15 minutes until her first violin lesson. She got a speeding ticket.

Continuing home after she was ticketed, she said, "It's your fault that I got a $50 speeding ticket."

I said, "I'm sorry Mom. You don't have to buy me any Christmas presents this year."

Mom said, "No, it's not your fault that I was speeding. You'll get Christmas presents."

My second grade teacher seemed to get me. He told my parents "I just let David be David." I really liked him.

In seventh grade we had to write a short paper about why we go to school. I pondered the question and wrote that I saw everyone sleeping and/or primping, so I came to the conclusion that everyone goes to school to show off their hair.

I was in trouble a bit in seventh and eighth grade. By ninth grade for some reason, I realized that now the grades really counted for my future: college and career. I still didn't care for school, but I applied myself and my parents were proud that I graduated with a cumulative 3.75 GPA. I was offered the chance to be in Advanced Placement (AP) math classes, but declined because I'd rather be able to pull an "easy" "A" in a regular class than have to work hard to get a "B" in an AP class. However, I really liked Spanish so I took three years of AP Spanish.

Perhaps I would have liked school better if I could have gone to Boise High. Several of my friends went there, and the atmosphere was more relaxed and more accepting. I felt there were more students at Boise High like myself who "danced to the beat of a different drummer." No one cared if your clothes weren't stylish, you had green hair and tattoos (which my parents wouldn't let me have anyway), or if you weren't a jock. I was small when I entered Capital High in the 10th grade and was teased by some jocks because of it. However, the girls loved my size and thought I was cute. One girl wrote in my year book: "Keep growin' Dave." I think I topped 100 pounds and 5'0" when I entered 10th grade, and 5' 7 ½" and 130 pounds by my senior year---all of it lean and mean of course.

***

When I was in fourth through sixth grade, Mom was working on her master's degree in social work. At that time Boise didn't have an MSW program, so she commuted four hours each way to Walla Walla College in Washington every week. She left Monday mornings and returned Wednesday or Thursday afternoons while Dad held down the fort in Boise. A couple of times each winter we traveled to Walla Walla on the weekends and stayed at her apartment, so Mom didn't have to drive over "The Blues" every week in the winter. I was proud of my mom and supportive of her studies and endeavors.

My grandparents came to visit us from Denver for Christmas one time; every other year we went to Denver to visit them. There can be some nasty snowstorms in Utah, Wyoming, and Colorado at this time of year so we took Amtrak. Amy and I had a lot of fun on those 20-hour trips, walking up and down the length of the train, while Mom knitted and read. We ate in the dining car and slept in our seats. Often Denver had 10 inches of snow so we'd have a beautiful white Christmas. I got to see my cousins, aunts and uncles, as well as my grandparents. When we gathered for Christmas dinner there were as many as 17 people around the table.

In addition to camping, we took various trips in the summers. One time we went to Lagoon Amusement Park near Salt Lake City. Two summers we went to Telluride, a beautiful town in southwestern Colorado. The elevation was 9000 feet and boasted breathtaking waterfalls. Mountain peaks of 13,000 feet surrounded the little town on three sides. My mother loved this town of 500 people (in the 1950's) and spent seven summers there as a child.

A trip to California when I was 13 was the most memorable trip for me. Amy had recently been to Disneyland with her school choir and wanted to stay home with a friend, so Dad, Mom, and I went to Disneyland and Universal Studios. The most fun thing in LA for me was a dinner show in a castle called Medieval Times. The dinner was 13th century style, with no eating utensils---every teen boy's dream, eating food with your fingers! Along with bibs came paper crowns and banners; there were two teams, and your banner indicated which team you were to cheer for. A short play was presented with kings, queens, knights, sword fights, and horse jousting.

Next we drove south to Palm Desert to stay at Dad's cousin's beautiful home which had a swimming pool. She lived in Alaska and wintered in Palm Desert. After a couple of relaxing days it was onward to San Diego; we went to Sea World and to the San Diego Zoo. Dad and I did some body surfing in the ocean and got to surfboard too. We also crossed the border into to Tijuana for the day.

I had two memorable trips to visit my Bromfield grandparents and sail with them in the San Juan Islands. When I was eight we met them in Seattle, then went to Point Roberts, Washington to sail in their 32-foot sailboat, "Sweet Seasons." The boat had living quarters below deck. When my grandparents retired, they spent 10 summers sailing the San Juans. Grandpa learned to sail when he was a teenager in Long Island, New York, before he moved to Tucson in his senior year of high school, where he met my grandma. While they attended the University of Arizona, they married when Grandpa was drafted into service during World War II at age 20. After ten years they sold the boat and became "snowbirds," wintering in Safford, Arizona, 130 miles northeast of Tucson.

When I was 13 I traveled by myself on Amtrak, leaving Boise at 4:00 a.m. I had an enjoyable 15 hour ride to Seattle where Grandpa and Grandma met me. We went day sailing in Canada the first day and went cruising the next three days. At first the waves were huge and I was nervous, but things calmed down after awhile and I got used to it. While cruising we saw a seal swim next to the boat; we also saw dolphins doing tricks for us. I got to row around in the dinghy by myself and fish.

# Chapter 4

## Fainting

Wrestling was one of the junior high sports I was involved in. I lettered in that sport through Capital High School when I was a Freshman. In February 1994 while sprinting around the gym during warm up, I fainted. Evidently I stopped breathing. The sports medic performed mouth-to-mouth resuscitation on me and I started breathing again. The ambulance was called. The wrestling coach's son called home and notified Mom.

About ten minutes later Mom stepped into the ambulance crying and upset, which embarrassed me. I was trying to hide the fact that I was worried. The paramedic told her to calm down, which didn't sit well with her. He also said, "Your son fainted while sprinting; he stopped breathing and had a small seizure, which can be common in an incident like this." By then Dad had arrived. The ambulance took me to the hospital emergency room. My parents followed in their car.

They drew my blood at the hospital and ran some other tests. After an hour or so they deemed me ready to go home, with appropriate follow up by my pediatrician and the pediatric cardiologist I had been seeing every three years since I was born. In the two or so weeks that followed I was given several medical tests. The last test they gave me was called a "tilt-table" test. They strapped me to a table; then injected me with something like adrenaline, devised to get my pulse rate raised quickly. Next they tilted the table to an upright position. My head began lolling and my eyes were rolling back. I felt slightly nauseous and was about to pass out. The doctor called out, "Stop!" They put the table down, stopped the injection and I didn't pass out. It was not a pleasant experience. Mom told me she cried because she hated seeing me about ready to pass out.

The doctor said, "This test confirms David has a condition known as neurocardiosyncope." Normally when a person exercises or exerts themselves, the heart rate increases and the blood pressure goes up concurrently. In my case the pulse increased but my blood pressure dropped dramatically which can result in fainting. What worried mom (and me frankly) was that at wrestling practice I stopped breathing. What if I had been out by myself, fainted and stopped breathing and no one was there? Would I have started breathing on my own?

The doctor said, "This syndrome is not uncommon in teens, and most of them grow out of it." He reminded me to always warm up before exercising and prescribed a blood pressure medicine. I took it a short while but didn't like the side effect of feeling light headed. Light headedness (fainting) was the same thing they were trying to treat with the medication, so I saw no point in taking it anymore.

The doctor told Mom to bring me back in three years for an echocardiogram and if all looked well he could discharge me. The coach wanted a doctor's note before I could return to wrestling. On March 22, 1994 the doctor wrote a note which said: "David may wrestle". The season was over anyway, and I elected not to continue in wrestling the following year. The next year I did experience light headedness from time to time while participating in various sports. Mom kept her parents informed of all the drama, and my grandma Bromfield wrote to Mom: "We are so glad the final test seems to have given the doctors the cause of his recent problems, and that it can be controlled with medication and proper precautions on David's part. That is quite a relief."

Three years later I had an echocardiogram. Mom and I both watched my heart pumping on the monitor. According to the doctor nothing looked wrong with my heart. That was a relief to both of us. He said I could do any sport I wanted, but reminded me to always "warm up." He said, "The army may not take you because of this condition." Even though I was in ROTC in the ninth grade, I was no longer interested in the military; so that pronouncement was no big disappointment to me. As Mom would say, she thinks I joined ROTC because I liked uniforms.

# Chapter 5

### Learning to Roll

Dad was one of the early Idaho pioneer whitewater kayakers, back in the day (1970's) when they had to battle with long, inflexible plastic boats. He kayaked the Payettes and other rivers with Keith Taylor, Tulio Celano, Roger Hazelwood, and a couple of trips with the famed Dr. Walt Blackadar of Salmon, Idaho. Some of the wives also kayaked a bit, including Betsy Hazelwood and Dawn Taylor. Mom preferred shuttle bunny duty.

Dad and his buddies were the extreme kayakers of their day; I'm in awe of what they accomplished. They pushed the limits on exciting expeditions. Dad was impacted pretty deeply when he witnessed a middle-aged man on one trip get stuck in his long kayak between two boulders. They were kayaking the East Fork of the South Fork of the Salmon, which starts near Yellow Pine, Idaho. Although the kayaker's head was above water, the water was rushing over his nose and mouth. The men tried valiantly to get him out quickly, but it took a long time. With two physicians on the trip, once the kayaker was out of the water, CPR was performed, but he didn't make it. In addition, the legendary Walt Blackadar and a young friend of Walt's both drowned in two different kayak accidents a couple of years later. About that time Mom and Dad were expecting their second child--- me. Dad took a long leave of absence from kayaking as he felt he was beginning to push the limits of his expertise and wanted to be around to raise his family.

Dad had the honor of the largest rapid on the main Payette bearing his name. He paddled into this rapid, got stuck in the same spot, and had to swim on at least two different trips, so Keith, Tulio, and Roger named it "Mike's Hole." People were impressed to find out I was the child of the namesake of this rapid.

Dad was 42, athletic, and in very good shape when I was born. He still enjoyed a good adventure. Once he went parasailing over the bay in Acapulco. After he was in the air he noticed how old and frayed the equipment looked, and was a bit nervous about that. Another time he went on a crop duster ride in the Mountain Home area. It was a rickety old plane with an open cockpit and Dad was seated hanging out over the edge of the opening. He got to take the wheel of the plane for awhile. The pilot did some loops and Dad had the time of his life.

I inherited a thrill-seeking nature from Dad. He loved to ski, hunt, hike, play tennis and racquetball, and of course, kayak. Dad and I did all of those things together. When we hunted chukkar together, our dog Jenny was in "dog heaven" as she ran up and down hills chasing the birds.

About the time I was 13 Dad took up kayaking again. He renewed old friendships with the Taylors and the Hazelwoods, and made some new friends with kayakers Barry and Maria Eschen, Gary Payne and others. He took things a bit slower as he was now in his mid-fifties. After watching Dad kayak for about a year, and after my recent scare incident while wrestling, I wanted to try something else. I said, "Dad, I'd like to learn to kayak." I think Dad had this in mind all along so he could have a companion to kayak with when others weren't available.

He bought me a blue Dancer--- one of those long boats--- for $100 in late spring of 1994. The next year I upgraded to a $250 used kayak. I was 14 going on 15 when Dad took me over to Aunt Susan's swimming pool and taught me to roll. I learned to roll in less than 20 minutes, both sides. I was stoked. We went to the Boise River on

other days, and I kept working on my roll and padd'
took some swims the first year or two; I hated havi—

On August 28, 1994 my love affair with the river and kayaking
was sealed. I took my first trip down the Main Payette with Dad and
had a blast. We went past Mike's Hole without incident. Dad took
Amy and me down the Main the summer before in a $1.00 small raft
he bought at a garage sale. He loved garage sales and was probably
about as tight with his money as I was, which is where I inherited
that trait too. The boat was not the best, and leaking like a sieve. Into
Mike's Hole we went, and Amy fell into the river and freaked out.

I was glad that I wasn't following in Dad's footsteps and going to
have to swim or take a thrashing in Mike's Hole. However in my first
year or two, I did take a few swims from time to time. I was too
young yet to be able to (legally that is) "drink beer from a bootie"---a
kayaker's way of paying penance for taking a swim.

The following spring, in celebration of Maria Eschen's 50th
birthday, we were invited along on a four-day trip down the Lower
Owyhee River. This was May 1995, shortly after my 16th birthday.
The Eschens knew how to organize a trip; Maria authored a book
called *River Otter: Handbook for Trip Planning* [3]. The food was
excellent and we all pitched in with camp duties. We camped at a hot
springs and took turns soaking our tired shoulders and backs. I spent
a lot of time playing in an eddy near by the camp, and learning
maneuvers such as "endos" and "pirouettes."

As Maria tells it I was Dad's shadow in the early days. She states
that in the exploration of the upper reach of the Middle Fork of the
Payette, I decided to portage around the "BMW" (Barry, Mike, and
Werner) rapid somewhere below Hardscrabble Camp. That was the
beginning of my young kayak career, showing judgment and respect
for the water--- knowing when to portage a situation that I felt I
wasn't ready for. Instead I played trip photographer and took shots
of Barry in the rapid and other shots as well. She inscribed a copy of
her *River Otter* book to me with, "David, you may be dangerous to
some, but to me you will always be the essence of the wild river

...the one sliding down the 20-foot bank into a gnarly hole---
only to surface laughing his head off."

In July 1996, I had one more nine day trip with a group that also
included the Eschens and several of my mom's colleagues. I had a
playboat this trip. Besides playing in waves, I jumped off cliffs into
the water. The adults commented that I had no fear.

The trip was fun. I loved the river. But I was ready to branch out
with a younger group of kayaking friends. I think Dad was about to
lose his son as companion/kayaker since I had surpassed his kayaking
ability within one year. He knew that day was soon to come. I'm very
thankful for his mentoring, teaching me the basics, and introducing
me to my life's passion.

# Chapter 6

## Becoming a Man

Every young boy strives and aspires to be a man like his father. Becoming a man means finally making decisions for yourself, strutting with confidence, and for me, tackling Class V. When anyone takes on Class V, it's a big endeavor, but when a boy of 15 crosses that line it's a significant definition of the boy's character. Unknowingly I had approached that day, and what a day it would be.

The Milner Section of the Snake River, near Twin Falls, Idaho, is described in the guidebooks as the "most powerful Class V in Idaho." It's enormous and only the top experts should attempt this section of river. "When winter snows overfill the reservoirs, the gates are thrown open," resulting in some huge water. At this time it is "one of the best big water runs in Idaho, being full of massive waves and holes you can get lost in." [4]

Dad said, "Wake up sleepy head. It's Easter morning; time to get ready for church." Stretching and rubbing my eyes, I peered out the window. What an incredible day it was. The sun glimmered above the mountains--- its rays uninterrupted through the sky.

I walked into the kitchen and there on the table Mom had placed my usual Easter basket filled with yellow Peeps, one largish chocolate bunny, a Cadbury egg, and my favorite jelly bellies. Slowly I started waking up after a pancake, scrambled eggs, bacon and orange juice breakfast. The more I woke up the more I started to get pumped for the day. Today I was going to paddle a new river then watch some incredible boaters run an amazing piece of whitewater.

I got my gear together and started heading for the door. Dad asked, "Are you getting ready for church?" Seeing that I was holding all my paddling gear his face saddened. "Today's Easter Sunday, David." But seeing the excitement in my eyes he nodded his head in approval of my departure. I was out the door.

The plan for the day was to boat a section of the Malad River that was on the way to the Class V Milner Section of the Snake River. We would all boat this short Class IV stretch then proceed on to the Milner where I would watch two friends boat this treacherous piece of whitewater. The Milner Section was pumping at an incredible 20,000 cfs that day, a level it rarely reached. With the canyon walls constricting in and the gradient dropping an astounding 100 feet in this mile of the Snake River, it made a very impressive, but short stretch of water. I was going with two Class V boaters that I really respected. These guys had been paddling this type of water for years, something I'd only seen in magazines up to this point. Joel being the older and more experienced of the two, had paddled the stretch before and was really excited to do it again and introduce it to other paddlers.

The two-hour drive to the river seemed incredibly long. As usual we talked about all things boating: stories, details, jokes, rivers, people---all my favorite things to talk about. I heard about someone who died on this stretch in the past. There was no room for mistakes; a swim here could easily have a fatal ending. I was impressed that these guys were going to paddle it and felt honored that I would be able to witness it.

The warm up river was a lot of fun. Early season, blazing sun, warm weather---simply perfect. But it was short and left me feeling unfulfilled. We boated it twice then headed on to the next portion of our plan.

Upon arrival we scampered up and down the river scouting it from the canyon rim. It looked huge, even from our far off vantage point. The more I looked at the river and lines that the two talked about paddling the more I could see myself doing those same lines. I visualized all the moves, the entire mile of river in my head. It was flawless. Ride the large waves at the top, round the corner, head right to avoid a school bus sized pour over, punch through incredible diagonals while heading back center. Paddle, paddle, paddle hard to make it through a river wide V-wave known as the "Wall of Water", then stay off the canyon walls where the water would treat you like driftwood until the take-out, which would be in sight by this time. It was short and would be a fast, adrenalizing run.

We talked it over and scouted it in its entirety for a long time, building the juices within. I still believed I was capable of doing this amazing river. But did I have the skill, the power? I was only 15 and I was thinking about doing something that usually only men do in their prime. Was I ready to take that step into the things I had read about in books and magazines? "I'm definitely not an expert by any means, possibly someday though," I thought. But there has to be one defining moment, one transition day where a person crosses that line into the dangerous realm of Class V. It was hard to believe, but I had finally reached that day without even knowing it.

After much consideration the younger of the two said he wasn't going to paddle it. It was over his head and simply scared him. Joel's hopes were broken. He had been looking forward to paddling this stretch again for a number of years. I stepped forward and spoke up confidently. "I'll paddle it with you." Their eyes perked up. This was something unexpected to them, but in the back of their minds they had known that this transition day would soon come for me.

More talking and scouting continued to boost my confidence as we scouted every inch of the river. More importantly I understood the consequences facing me. I gave it some more thought to make sure what I was feeling was the right thing for me to do. The decision had to be made by myself alone---I was going to paddle this river. Whether it would be my last or my first in a life full of Class V experiences was soon to be discovered.

Gearing up, I remained calm and quiet. "You feeling good about this, David?" Joel asked. The nod of approval went out to him as we pushed into the moving water. We stopped to surf a wave at the top to help warm up and relieve a little tension. Two more strokes and we were committed. The water moved faster than I had ever gone in a kayak; 20,000 cfs roaring under me, pounding on the canyon walls, thundering all around me. But I was in my element and ready for anything that would come my way. I was right on Joel's tail but following my own line and only watching him for potential flaws and changes in the water and to my line.

The crux of the run was upon me, a river wide wall of water that marked the end or beginning of my Class V career. Looking forward I saw the competent paddler's boat ahead tumbling in the frothing mess, end over end. No time to be scared, I charged into it, my blades flashing left, right, left, right. The wall hit me hard knocking me onto my back deck stopping my boat then shooting me high into the air and out of the mess. I rolled quickly and paddled hard to the take-out, cresting and crashing on the frothing, breaking waves. No carnage from that one, just my aching cheeks from grinning so much. My run had been better than Joel's.

Only six minutes of paddling but what a wild ride. It was now official. Easter Sunday, April 16, 1995, like my father and the men that accompanied me, I became a man. Let the confidence shine through, decisions be made quickly and clearly, and most importantly, let the ladies come swarming.

# Chapter 7

## Dan Menten and Andrew West

Early on in high school I met two guys who would become my best friends, Andrew (Dru) West and Dan Menten. I met Dru at the Rodeo at Otter Slide campground about four miles north of Banks, Idaho on Highway 55. I was 15 and he was 14. Dru and I had signed up for the slalom race category in the Payette Whitewater Roundup; I also volunteered for river safety support at the event. I saw this young kayaker who was competing in the slalom event, doing a great job. I was rocking a blue/gray wool hat Dad had given me and my studded belt. Dru especially noticed my belt and said "Kewl belt, dude!" He had a Moon Ska record label sticker on his boat and I asked him about it. He said he got it at a show featuring one of his favorite bands, The Toasters. I was also a fan of Ska music and over the years we listened to countless hours of Ska while driving around the country in search of fun and adventure.

After talking a short while Dru and I realized we were about the same age, same level of boating skill and the same level of coolness. We liked to skateboard, ski, and snowboard, and both of us had a rebellious attitude. Dru eagerly agreed when I asked him if he wanted to go surf, so we loaded up the boats and headed out to check some of the local play waves, ending up at the Main Payette. Long since washed out by a landslide, it was a fun wave and well suited to the boats of the day. The water levels weren't the best for the wave that day but we had fun and recognized an important kinship. Thus our friendship began.

I was going on 17 and Dan was still 15 when I met him. Dan and Dru were cruising up to the Payette River for a paddling session. They saw a bunch of kayakers at the Bank's parking lot and pulled over to see what was going on. Dru and I had already met. I went up to them and said, "Let's go paddle the North Fork!" Dan later told me he noted my unkempt hair and observed a "Chihuahua-like little man complex" at what he considered my posturing. However we soon became fast friends and kindred spirits.

I became a fixture at Dru's house, and his parents, Anne and Jim West, didn't seem to mind that whenever I was there I helped myself to whatever food I could find. Dan's family also kindly let me take advantage of the open door/open fridge policy, which meant that when walking through their front door I said, "hi" on my way to the kitchen and the sandwich ingredients. I needed those carbs for fueling my small but wiry body with the energy needed to kayak.

\*\*\*

Dan was known as DanRA because he was always a Run Away from home when he boated. This set the standard for Dan, Dru and me to have as much fun as possible while boating, including the drives to and from our location. Though when we got home we knew it would not be pleasant. This isn't to say our parents didn't want us kayaking---they liked the idea of our boating to keep us out of trouble---but we had excelled so rapidly that they were worried. In addition, the three of us brought out some craziness in one another. We became known around the local scene as the most unpredictable, well-rounded, and funnest paddlers. [5]

The inception of "D-Cubed" came about when Dan, Dru and I, ---three D's---worked on a video together. Our first attempt at a small video was titled *Gardena Derby*, a sort of underground video production. It was named after a short stretch of Highway 55, near the little "town" of Gardena, slightly north of Horseshoe Bend. Known by little and seen by only a select few, it was a low-budget precursor to the Young Guns movies of the early 2000's. Using the roughest of editing equipment we managed to bring the spectacle of 10,000 cartwheels (the hottest new move at the time) to the dizzied and slightly nauseous viewer. When it came time for the infamous crash and burn segment, *Gardena Derby* viewers were treated with one shot after another of me getting spanked in my yellow Acrobat 270. I took a log to my chest on Hazard Creek, sometimes running drops upside-down. The film culminated with a sweet shot of my 45 second, adrenaline sucking beatdown in Jaws Rapid on the North Fork. Despite this, we always emerged unscathed at the bottom. [6]

The three of us were so fired up about paddling; we never backed out of a planned trip. However, when other friends wanted to back out of a trip, they may have been put off by my strong attitude. I'd take their gear, load it in the rig, chastise them for being lazy and drive them up the river.

In the spring of 1997, the year after the three of us met, we went on a road trip with Jordan Dew, and Brett Gleason. Dan skipped a week of school, it was his junior year, but I had graduated. Dan told me the trip helped define who he would become. We paddled The Little White Salmon River, near Portland. I went deep off of Spirit Falls, about a 35-footer, my first large drop. I lost my paddle and got shoved behind the falls into a cave. Dan and the others retrieved my paddle and roped it down to me in the cave. By that time I was sitting out of my boat on a large log. Dan said I had an unforgettable look on my face. I was upset at myself for the bad line off the falls. Later we drove to California, paddled in the Redwoods and made a big loop back up into Oregon.

A couple years later Dru and I really missed Dan when he left for college in California. We did however go to visit and paddle together on the Cal Salmon and other rivers including the day we went down Bridge Creek in a lightning fast four hours. Dan and Dru raised their eyebrows when I said, "None of the drops were big enough."

# Chapter 8

## Senior Year of High School

My first car was a brown 1980 Honda station wagon which my folks bought for me. I outfitted it with the requisite punk-rock tape player and "OIL" stickers covering the back window. I built a homemade kayak rack using aluminum rods and attached it to the roof with bailing wire and a stacker built from 2x4's. It wasn't beautiful but it got me to the river.

During my last semester of high school I had a class that gave credits for having a job. This was my ideal concept of school, leave early and earn money at the same time. I did well at my office job and they liked me, but it wasn't my thing. Also that winter I began my first association with the raft-making company AIRE and worked off and on for them until 2003. This was a great job. The owner Greg Ramp allowed me the flexibility to work when I was in town, and leave when I had to go kayaking. I did my best to represent the company while I was on the road at kayak rodeos and on tours, talking to shops and raft companies.

High school graduation finally arrived in May 1997. Yippee! My grandparents from Denver came and my family hosted a party for me at our house. We had a Baskin Robbins ice cream cake and a good time with my dog Jenny in on the festivities as well. Everyone gave me camping gear, which was a creative idea since I camped a lot on my kayaking trips

Mom sang Elgar's *Pomp and Circumstance* all week. She told me she loved that tune, and got teary-eyed at graduations, starting with her own graduation ceremony from Golden (Colorado) High School in 1965. Yep, my mom was weird sometimes. She teared up a bit as I walked across stage to receive my diploma. My parents of course filmed the occasion. My good friend Dustin Urizar met up with me afterwards and we went partying.

A couple of weeks after graduation we had a family meeting and my parents announced to Amy and me that they were getting a divorce later that summer. They had decided to wait until after my graduation so as not to put a downer on my last couple of months in high school. I was pretty upset about it at first but soon came to realize it was best for them. They remained on cordial terms after the divorce. Mom stayed in the house that first year, and I expressed a desire to stay "with the house" as well.

I earned my raft-guiding license early in the summer, but never guided a raft. I was a safety boater for a short while for Cascade Raft and Kayak Company. I rescued a girl out of the South Fork on one of our trips, after she took a swim. Later I was let go for hanging out with a female employee and visiting her at Otter Slide Campground. She was 16. I had barely turned 18. This was the only job I ever got fired from.

I wasn't going to start college for one year in order to work and save money to minimize the impact of student loans. My parents thought it was a good idea anyway for a young man of 18 to have a year to mature before starting college. I worked at Good Times burger joint full-time during the winter and saved up a good bit of money for college. It wasn't all work though. I had an awesome time snowboarding at Bogus Basin Ski Resort as often as I could.

Dru and I spent a lot of time together that summer of '98. He was driving an older model red Mercedes Benz, which really impressed the girls. We both got sponsored that summer--- Dru by Perception and myself by Pyranha. I was totally amazed and excited.

# Chapter 9

## Riding the Rails with Tyler

I met my good friend Tyler Smith during my sophomore year; we hung out a lot with various friends including Dustin Urizar, Aaron Maxie, Byl Kravatz, Richie Howard, Donelle Mackey, Skyler, and Marcus Pierce among others. This was a group of "non-kayaking" friends; some of us were skateboarders; some of us were into break dancing. Some had numerous tattoos and body piercings; some had long spiked green hair in a Mohawk style. Despite the wild and crazy look, many of these friends were in Advanced Placement (AP) classes at school.

My parents wouldn't let me get green Mohawk hair so I conceded to expressing my individuality in a slightly less extreme manner by bleaching my hair blonde, sometimes more orange in shade; later I dyed it black, which was the closest to my true color at that age. I had one pierced ear for a short while. And I had a secret tattoo on my back; a homemade one, which I got at a party one time. Later I had ankle tats with waves and checkers, two different Ska guys, and the words "OIL/H2O." Each leg represents different aspects of my life. It all comes down to oil and water.

Tyler and I and our respective girlfriends at the time went to the prom. I also went to a homecoming dance sporting my dad's tux which was too big, a big bow tie of his, and short one inch hair which I tried to spike with the aid of some hair mousse. To that dance I took my girlfriend, Kasia Mastas. Kasia and I remained good friends and later dated again in 2003.

Tyler and I formed a punk band, "Wrong Time, Wrong Place," and made our own cassette tape--- all original songs. We both played guitar and we invited a friend from my high school to play bass. I'm sure the bass player didn't want to be in our band very long because he was highly talented and went on to get a degree in music. Nevertheless we played loudly, venting our teen age frustrations and were able to release a lot of pent up energy.

Tyler had been hopping trains with Ronne, another friend of his, for two years since age 17. In early summer of 1998 he asked if I wanted to join them for an adventure. I was stoked for the experience. His faithful dog Hooker, a three-year-old black lab/spaniel mix, always accompanied them on these trips. We had our sleeping bags in our backpacks. We hopped the train in Nampa, which had low security, so we could hide out under the wheels of the train before it started, or in a bucket car. The train was headed for Portland with us, our gear, and Hooker, safely or not so safely resting on a platform beneath one of the cars. There wasn't enough space to sit up, but we could lean on our elbows or lie back and watch the country go by with a cool breeze in our faces.

Tyler and Ronne knew the ropes. Portland had a lot of security so we had to hop out of the train at a state park near Portland where the train slowed down quite a bit. Hooker was always anxious and we had to coax her and gently throw her off. She learned to hit the ground running after the first try. We'd throw our backpacks and gear off first, and when we finally de-boarded we had to walk back a ways to retrieve everything. By that time we looked pretty scruffy but managed to hitchhike into town where we could stay a couple of days.

We returned to the same state park, hiding out under a nearby bridge until the train slowed enough for us to hop on. This time the train took us to Pocatello, Idaho. We stayed with friends for a couple of days and then decided to go to Denver. You never really knew where you might end up, as sometimes the front and/or the back of the train would be leading the way. If it was a long train we really couldn't tell where we were headed. Instead of Denver we ended up going back to Boise again. I got off there and called it a day for this adventure because the whitewater was calling me, but I had a blast with Ronne and Tyler. In all on that trip, we traveled over 1400 miles.

Tyler put on many miles this way and I often thought he should write a book about it. He had shared with me some of the highlights of his adventures. Sometimes they'd have to run and catch the train, one of them carrying the dog on his shoulders because she was frightened by the speed of the train. Ronne and Tyler threw their gear on a car and by the time they both got on, they often ended up on different cars. Sometimes they weren't able to get back to the same car and meet up again until the next train stop.

Once Tyler was running to catch a train with Hooker on his back when he caught a ladder but slipped off. The boxcar behind this particular car hit him in the back and sent him flying, thankfully, away from the train and not under it. Tyler relates that on the axle of a train wheel are three bolts. As the wheels begin to turn faster and those three bolts begin to blur, the train is moving too fast to hop onto. Tricks of the trade in case you ever want to try this.

Tyler and Ronne started adding more luxuries for their trips: a butane stove, gallon of water, of course dog food, a couple of books, a tape player, and one time a hammock. They'd tie it underneath the car (with their gear and dog on the platform beneath the car), and take turns resting, swinging along in the breeze as they watched the scenery fly by. They traveled south in the winter, north in the summer. They traveled back to Manhattan and landed a job once as extras on a TV show. They each got $50 and they thought they were living high.

They only got caught once, in a little town in northeast Wyoming called Gillette. At the time the town had a population of about 8000 people. They were sitting on the edge of an open box car, slowly coming into town, their legs dangling out of the train, when they were spotted by a local waiting for the train to pass. He called the police and they were arrested, spending two nights in jail. Thinking perhaps they were run-aways, their parents were contacted, and the parents said they knew where their sons were and it was okay with them. The dog was put up at the local veterinarian's office while Tyler and Ronne were in jail. All charges were dropped, and after some notoriety with their pictures and the story on the front page of the Gillette newspaper, they were on their way back home, via railroad. It might have been the most exciting thing that had happened in that town for the last decade. Tyler and Ronne never joined the gang FTRA (Freight Train Riders of America), which had some pretty dangerous train hopping initiations. They remained independent train hoppers, or as they might have been called in the old days, hobos.

# Chapter 10

## A Wedding, Then off to College

In early May 1998 my parents and I took a trip to Fort Collins, Colorado for Amy's graduation from Colorado State University (CSU). She graduated with a degree in Microbiology; I was proud of my sister. I was happy to be there for that event, and the party that my grandparents gave for her afterwards.

Amy had become engaged to Travis earlier that spring. Mom and Amy were busy arranging and coordinating a wedding long distance since Amy was in Fort Collins and the wedding was to be in Boise. On August 23 the wedding was held outdoors at the "Bishop's House," an old Victorian house in east Boise by the foothills. The reception was indoors.

Mom tried to get me to comb and part my hair in a more conventional style for the event. I didn't want to comb it as, unbeknownst to her, I was starting to work on some "dreads." Amy intervened, pulled Mom aside and said, "Let it go mom, his hair looks okay." I did don the tux though and read a poem during the ceremony. Later Amy and I danced. It was a fun reception.

The day after the wedding my parents were taking me to Durango where I would start college. It was a very busy and hectic time, with mixed blessings for Mom. She was losing a daughter but gaining a son-in-law, and she was losing a son to college in another state. For the first time she would be an empty nester, what she tells me is that longed for time in a parent's life that is sometimes difficult and sad at first.

\*\*\*

I had received a four-year WICHE scholarship (Western Interstate Exchange Student Scholarships) of $5000 per year to attend Ft. Lewis College in Durango. It's near Telluride in the San Juan Mountains, in southwestern Colorado. Why did I pick Durango you might ask? Because Colorado has great kayaking, and Durango has an awesome river, the Animas (soul, spirit), running right through the middle of town. Plenty of time to kayak after classes every day before dark. Also it was a good college with only 3,700 students.

I had been packing all week for the move to Durango. Monday, August 24, 1998, we loaded my stuff and kayaks into two cars, my Dad's station wagon and my old Honda station wagon. I would follow Mom and Dad in my car. As my parents were about to pull out, I said I'd be following them in a few minutes and would meet them at Burley where I-84 heads south to Salt Lake City.

I was leaving Boise for the first time in my 19 years and wanted to have a moment alone in the house. I especially wanted to be alone to say good bye to Jenny my dog, who I was going to miss very much. I will admit I had a bit of a tearful good bye. Leaving home for the first time is a momentous occasion in any young man's life. Ambivalent feelings about leaving and starting something new. Am I taking the right path? All sorts of questions went through my head. Was this more my parents' dream for me rather than mine? I said my good byes, put Jenny in the back yard (she was being watched by the neighbors until Mom got home), locked the front door, and started out on my new adventure.

We met up and continued our little caravan to Durango, passing through Green River, Utah and Grand Junction, Colorado. Durango is approximately 730 miles from Boise. Mom wanted to spend the night in her favorite place in the world, Telluride, so we had a nice night there.

The next morning we set out bright and early for Durango, a two and one half-hour drive. There was a parent meeting at noon and some meetings and orientation for me to attend. I got in my "beater" Honda, and the engine wouldn't turn over no matter what we tried--- jumping the car, etc. Mom was more in a panic than I was, but it was a bummer. She wanted to be there in time for the meetings and such.

With Telluride being a small, isolated town, there wasn't much chance of getting any necessary parts in time if they were needed, so we began to look for a tow truck to take my car over the mountain pass for a reasonable price and would leave right away. We found a tow truck driver and started off on the breath-taking drive over Lizard Head Pass on CO Highway 145 with its stunning scenery of the San Juan Mountains. The beautiful peaks exceeded 14,000 feet in elevation. We passed Lizard Head peak on the right, aptly named for its shape. My mom used to camp in this area with her family as a child. My grandpa had a Ph.D. in geology and worked for the United States Geological Survey (USGS). He mapped this territory for several years. We continued past the little towns of Dolores and Cortez, and past the entrance to Mesa Verde, which I visited later in the year.

We arrived in Durango about 11:00 a.m. The college was on a bluff overlooking the Animas River and the city of Durango, with a population in 1998 of 13,000. The tow truck pulled right up to my dorm. I had to arrange to have the car fixed later. We quickly took my stuff into my dorm room---kayak and all. I eventually tied it to the ceiling, as the room was small. Tyson, my roommate, wasn't there yet.

We went to our separate meetings. Afterwards we met again. My parents were ready to leave. I wanted them to stay longer, but Mom and Dad said they had to be on their way to Denver to see Grandpa-- -my mother's dad. Also the next evening they would be attending another wedding reception in the Longmont area near Denver, hosted by Amy's new in-laws for their Colorado relatives that couldn't make it to the Boise wedding.

It was tough saying good-bye to my parents. Mom later confessed that as she and Dad drove away, they stopped the car to take one last look over the bluff down at the town. They cried just like they did when they left Amy for the first time at Colorado State University four years earlier.

I was going to major in engineering because I thought I could be a hydraulic engineer since I liked water. I took 15 credits the first semester including Pre-Calculus (math was always my best subject), computer aided drafting, Chemistry and Lab (which was *not* my favorite subject!), and First Aid, which was an easy A. My classes started at 8 a.m. every day, but that wasn't a problem for me. Except for Chemistry, the classes were easy. Best of all, my work-study job on campus was teaching kayaking in the college swimming pool.

The cafeteria food wasn't that great but it was filling, and I ate a lot of it. Foods I really missed though were my mom's tuna casserole (with chili powder--- I always added more than she cooked it with), hash browns, hotdogs, cheese, refried beans, and stuff. A friend Timmy probably thought I was crazy, as he saw me pile all kinds of stuff onto my plate every morning then mix a lot of Tabasco on it.

In general I found the town to be pretty boring if you were under 21. A lot of my friends were over 21, and they hung out in the bars where I couldn't join them. As soon as the snow flew, I got a reduced cost student pass to snow board at Telluride and other local ski areas. So that helped a lot.

Early on I was driving in downtown Durango with my kayak on my car. I didn't know very many people yet, and I saw a guy about my age with a kayak on top of his car. I stopped to talk with him about the kayaking. Turns out he was a junior at Ft. Lewis College. His name was Skip Armstrong, and he was soon to become a very good friend of mine. He also taught kayaking at the college.

I met a few girls, which was nice. One was a cute college girl who assisted me in the kayak teaching job at the college. We went out from time to time. One time we took a picnic lunch and hiked up to a beautiful little lake to go swimming.

During down time when I wasn't kayaking I listened to music and watched some TV. In addition to Ska, some of the music I liked was Bob Marley and other Reggae music, punk rock and some Johnny Cash. I also shared my mom's appreciation for classical music. I especially liked Mozart, Beethoven, and Bach. She gave me some of those CDs, so I listened to them on my headache days. The few times I did watch TV my favorite shows were *Saturday Night Live*, *Simpsons*, and especially *Seinfeld*. However, sitting still long enough to watch TV was never really my thing.

Every day after class I'd head out to the Animas River before winter socked us in with snow. There was a play hole in the Smelter Rapid at Santa Rita Park, just five minutes from campus. In the spring, bigger waves and holes formed downstream, but in the fall, this was all Durango had to offer in terms of playboating. I often went with Timmy. We'd boat there sometimes well past dark.

I met Molly, Tracy, and some other students early on. Molly and I did lab work together, and I was happy to help her with our computer drafting homework. We went down to the river and had fun swinging from a rope that was tied to a tree, and jumping in.

In September I went to Mesa Verde with a friend from Boise who was at Ft. Lewis. The serenity of that place is awesome. The Cliff Dwellings of the Anasazi Indians I had remembered from a trip there earlier with my family, but they never failed to impress.

In November Skip, some other friends and myself went on a three day/two-night river trip to Westwater Canyon, about 60 miles east of Moab. It's the first whitewater stretch of the Colorado River in Utah. There are several challenging rapids, including the Class IV Skull Rapid. The desert scenery was awesome; it is similar to Arches National Park. We launched late in the afternoon on Friday and the weather was beautiful for November---clear, calm, and quite warm. When we woke up it was snowing and really rad. When we were done, our kayaks were all frozen and there was ice on the raft. On the way home it started raining; as we got closer to home it turned to snow. I could have kicked myself for not bringing my camera on this trip, and made a vow from then on never to be without a camera.

That year I also bought my first video camera. It was at this point that I essentially began chronicling my life and adventures on video.

Winter comes pretty hard at these elevations (10,650), but I did get to snowboard at Telluride, Crested Butte, and Purgatory, which is a local ski resort about 30 minutes from Durango. We also boarded at Red Mountain Pass. Skip and other friends and I had an awesome boarding day in the latter part of April. The sun was shining and the air was cold and crisp. The snow was waist deep, a very soft powder. I pulled off my first 360's front and back, with some grabs. I tried a couple of front flips and stuff. We got some good photos of my friends and me doing the flips.

At Thanksgiving and on a couple of other times, I traveled to Denver to visit my grandparents and sometimes Amy and Travis who were living in the resort town of Breckenridge. I was a bit homesick and especially missed Jenny. I wished she could come live with me but I was too transient to have a dog, plus dogs aren't allowed in dorms and many apartments. I emailed home to make sure Mom was keeping the insulated doghouse warm with cedar chips, and making sure the roof didn't leak.

I had lots of ambivalence about this whole college thing. I began having doubts in October even though I'd only been there one month. Some days I was really stoked about it and others I wondered what I was doing there. I was good about studying, but I often got to the library to study then find out I'd left my books at the dorm. I did get good grades and had at least a B average by the end of the first semester. I told my mom not to get all worried and fussy about my ambivalence, and said things like, "I'll go for at least one year."

Mom advised me to take any courses I wanted second semester, anything that sounded interesting, and not worry about having to stay on a track like engineering. She told me to give it at least a year, as the first semester many students are homesick. Although I had the $5000 per year scholarship, which was great, and my parents were helping out, I had a small student loan of about $1000 a semester and my job. I guess I was naïve, but it finally hit me, "Duh!" Student *loan* means I pay it back someday. I guess I was thinking it was a grant or some such. I didn't want to accumulate much debt while in college.

Mom even said I could move into an apartment in town if it was the dorm that I didn't like. However, the dorm was not the issue. Mom was willing to work with me, and trying hard to sway me. She suggested I spend one year at Durango, then come back to Boise State where I could live at home, and my parents could foot most of the entire bill. All of these thoughts and ideas were going through my head, over and over, as I weighed what I wanted to do with my life and career.

Christmas break was coming, and I had to put some money down and make a reservation for the dorm room soon and make up my mind about whether I wanted to stay in school or not. I was up and down about this decision. Most of the up times had to do with the beauty of the Durango area, the kayaking, snowboarding, camping, hiking and such, and nothing to do with school itself. I really didn't want to be an engineer. I wanted to try to support myself so I could be a Kayaker.

December 1st, 1998, I sent an impassioned email straight from my heart, to my mother:

> Mom,
>
> I just don't see my future, or what I want to do with my life, consisting of school. I know I can make it if I want something bad enough. Trust me, I really want to have a good life so I will do everything in my power to make sure that happens.
>
> Unlike most people of this world, money and ordinary things don't fit into my life goals and plans. They are nice but I consider them luxury's [sic]. I have known for years that I was not like everyone else *and it is now time for me to put my life in perspective and start doing what I will be doing for the rest of my life. If I don't work on it now then everything will be lost.*
>
> *I must persue [sic] my dream of kayaking now; otherwise it will be too late.* I am almost 20 years old and I realize once I turn 20 I must be on my way for what will determine the rest of my

life. *This is why now is so critical.* If I go another semester I will have lost that much time and money towards reaching my goals. For the next few years I will have to be working towards my goals to make sure everything falls into place.

My life depends on the decisions that I make almost to this very day that could very possibly determine the outcome of my life. The time is now, so it is time to put my mind and body to work, it can't wait any longer…

I hope that whatever the outcome you and Dad will support my decision, no matter what it may be. Because support from a loving family is one of the best encouragements to me there is. I will pull through… I have done it up to now. Either college or kayaking will have the same result in the end…. The life that I will have to live with.

Love, Your Son,

David

I was hoping they would take this decision of mine well, but if they didn't I was going to pursue my dream anyway. Mom and Dad both were supportive of the idea. Probably they hoped that in a year or two I might go back to college, but for now I had their support and they wished me well in the pursuit of my dream of being a full-time kayaker…and whatever else I needed to do to help support that dream: various jobs, writing articles for kayak magazines, trying to get into professional kayak videos or maybe produce one of my own. I was willing to do whatever it took and happy to have the emotional support of my parents.

*** 

After spending Christmas in Boise with the family, I flew back to Durango and began to look for an apartment. Skip was renting a big house out of town aways, by a stream in the mountains. There was an extra bedroom so I moved in. Brian, Alex, and Lauren also lived there.

Molly and I had good times with Alex and Lauren pulling the kayaks down the hill behind the house to go boating, cooking dinners, and camping at places such as Navajo Reservoir. I really enjoyed the time Molly's family took me on a hot-air balloon ride in Denver.

By the end of April the owners of the house were returning and I had to find a new place to live. Molly invited me to live with her and two of her girlfriends in a three-bedroom duplex. Lucky guy. What else can I say?

I had a good job with Bomber Gear, a local kayak manufacturing company. I even got to be in some of their advertising booklets. This was the start of media exposure for me. If I was going to be sponsored I needed as much of it as possible.

Living in Durango did a lot to help me become a very good creek-boater. I hucked many drops while I was down there. I think I kayaked Vallecito Creek 12-14 times that year. It was one of my favorite creek runs and only required a one-mile hike-in.

Chad Crabtree was only 15 when I met him at the play wave on the Animas. He became a river rat at age 10 when his mother dropped him off daily one summer for kayaking lessons on the Animas River. Chad boated Vallecito with me a few times and other creeks as well. In 2001 I would meet up with him again, paddling in Costa Rica.

I met Toby Scarpella through Skip. Toby taught Skip how to roll. Toby and I took one of the coolest trips I've ever had down the Vallecito one time. We ended up kayaking in the dark with only the full moon to guide us. Toby and I did a second descent of Crazy-Woman Creek, a super-gnarly tributary of the upper Animas River. It's short and steep with four to five big drops. Not many boaters run it, due to its difficulty and also because it's on private property. Most boaters are averse to having shots fired at them, but we chanced it because it was such a great run. Sadly, Toby died in a kayaking accident in Canyon Creek in southwest Washington, March 2001.

By summer my dreads were long, tangled, and what my mom called obnoxious, as I hadn't shampooed since Amy's wedding the previous August. That's how you have to grow dreads, right? When the time came to get rid of them, I practically had to shave my head bald because the tangles were so bad. It was good to have "normal" hair again, and I know my parents agreed.

In April Mom asked if I'd like to meet up with her in Las Vegas for a three-day mini-vacation. She offered to pay my way, so I quickly accepted. I'd never been to Vegas, and I was stoked. She was meeting some friends from France who were visiting the States for the first time. There were no affordable commercial flights from Durango to anywhere, so I drove the 215 miles to Albuquerque, parked my car at the airport, and flew from there to Vegas where Mom met me.

We stayed at Treasure Island on the strip. We ate dinner on the top of the Stratosphere in a revolving restaurant, and Mom being prone to motion sickness became a bit nauseous. I wanted to take the thrill ride that goes from the top of the building down, but it was closed due to high winds. I was too young to gamble so I swam in the outdoor pools at our hotel, even though it was a bit chilly. We walked the strip and went to an awesome show.

That summer I traveled all around the country using Durango as my home base. I went to the Oregon Cup, Boise, Jackson Hole, back to Durango, to Boise again for three days, and to the Outdoor Retail Show in Salt Lake City to promote our upcoming video *The Revolution*. Next I went to West Virginia and North Carolina for seven weeks, then to Oregon again.

I had to work hard to line up sponsors. One very influential sponsorship that I landed the previous summer (98) was Pyranha, and I was pleased to be a part of their team. I gradually added other sponsors as well, such as Carrera, Smith, Ropegun, Necky, to name a few. Media exposure was one thing sponsors expected, and I got my first media exposure that year. Early in the summer Skip and I were kayaking La Plata Creek near Durango. There was a drop of about 20 feet through a very narrow chute. Skip took some fantastic photos of me kayaking down the drop. Bomber Gear used one of the photos in their 2000 catalog. In addition, *Kayak Magazine*, Spring 2001, used the photo and devoted a full page to it. Idaho River Sports (IRS), a kayak store in Boise, displayed a large poster, about 4x3 feet of that shot in their shop for several summers.

# Chapter 11

## Tornado

August 1999 was the second of several summers that I attended the Outdoor Sports Retail Trade Show in Salt Lake City. Between their winter and summer trade shows a crowd of 40,000 people often attended. It is the world's largest outdoor sports industry gathering. Retailers and media come together to market and sell products for outdoor sports, including North Face, Columbia, Timberland, Patagonia, Nike, and various kayak manufacturers, to name a few. Buyers include REI, Cabelas, Nordstrom's and many others. This was a perfect opportunity to network with potential sponsors, show teasers of the videos I was trying to market, etc. The retail show wasn't all about work. There was always a big party in the evening, not to be missed.

That year the show was held in two very large canvas tents. I was busy talking with a friend a little after noon on August 11, when we noticed it got really quiet. We looked around and saw that everyone was gone. Wondering what the heck was going on, we walked outside and saw a large black twister cloud coming our way! We ran to a near-by semi-truck and crawled under the truck in the nick of time. The tornado roared overhead. My heart pounded with adrenaline. I'd never been in a tornado before. Inch and a half hail stones smacked the pavement before our eyes and rattled the panels of the truck. Then suddenly everything went quiet. We stuck our heads out from under the truck to see the black clouds retreating. In retrospect, there had been dark clouds all day long.

The twister lasted about 15 minutes. It was rated an F2 tornado and cost Utah about $170 million. In addition there were 80 injuries and worse than that, one 38-year-old man from Nevada died; he'd had a booth at the retail show. Tornadoes are very rare in Utah. According to the news that night, it was among the most notable tornadoes to hit west of the Great Plains in the 20th century. The only other tornado in Utah with a fatality was in 1884. [7]

# Chapter 12

## West Virginia with Jordan Dew

Boating in West Virginia and North Carolina beckoned me. The rivers in that area, among them the Gauley, have a great rep for fantastic whitewater. Jordan Dew, a long-time raft guide and kayaker, and his girlfriend Suean and I decided to make the trip late in August 1999. We loaded our gear and their dog Millie into Suean's 1985 Toyota pick-up and headed back east. The truck already had 210,000 miles on it.

Our first stop was Littleton, Colorado where we stayed overnight at my grandparents' house. The rusty truck was in poor shape; we had to put blocks of wood behind the tires to keep it from rolling down the driveway into the street. My grandparents got a kick out of the vehicle, and wondered how we would make it the 4400 miles round trip between Boise and West Virginia and back. We were wondering too.

The good news is the truck made it to West Virginia--- barely. The bad news is that soon after we got there, it finally bit the dust. Suean then upgraded to a 1988 Dodge Caravan with only 115,000 miles on it for $600. Such a deal.

When we first arrived, between my job and setting up camp, I was running around from dawn to dusk. We set up camp in a place with electrical outlets for Suean's sewing machine, as she made a living sewing and selling clothing.

While at the Gauley River I made money being a video boater. Some days I had to be at work by 5:30 a.m. and didn't get back to camp until 8 or 9 p.m. Boarding the bus with the people who had paid for a trip, I worked to get them revved up for the adventure. It wasn't too hard because some of them had already been drinking. I kayaked ahead of raft trip groups, then took video of the biggest rapids from the bank of the river. During our lunch break I interviewed various people on film. At the end of the day I quickly edited a short video and hoped my salesmanship on the river was enough to sell them a video. I was making $85 per day plus $5 for every video I sold, netting as much as $230 in one weekend.

The Gauley River is dam controlled meaning water is released Friday through Monday, so I had the rest of the week off to boat and play in the river. Jordan and I boated a sweet Class V section of the lower Meadow River. I sprained a muscle in my wrist and had to ice it, but it was worth it. Some of the other rivers we boated were Cranberry, Upper Youghigen (I was quite discouraged on this hyped up river), Russell Fork, the Lower New and the sweet Green Narrows. We did some awesome creekin' too and ended up spending a fantastic seven weeks back east.

Two of the new kayaking buddies I met while at the Gauley were Leland Davis and Jay Moffatt. We also video boated together. We had an exciting time boating the Green River in North Carolina. Coming to the huge rapid, Gorilla, we got out to scout. Jay pointed out the standard line and went first to show us how it was done. As he approached the main falls of the rapid, he spun around and went backwards over Gorilla. I could hardly believe my eyes, but he was all right. I used this run later in my *Revolution* video.

Leland and I also boated in New York State before I left for home. Over the years Leland and I met up again at Salt Lake City and BC. When I rolled in at the Cheakamus parking lot in BC, I was stoked to see him. That day we watched some of a video I had developed in his van, before we went boating.

My plans for getting home were changing almost daily, but finally things worked out and I was able to go home with Jordan and Suean

in her new van. On the way back we boated near the
Virginia/Kentucky border as well as in the Asheville, North Carolina
area for a couple of days. Along the way I scored a free hotel,
although we did manage to scrape together $10 to give the owner.
Obviously we were all broke. We headed home through Oklahoma,
Texas, and eventually through Durango, Moab, and Salt Lake City.

When I got back to Boise, I had new digs. Mom and Dad had
decided Dad would keep our house and Mom bought a new three-
bedroom townhouse. She offered me a bedroom and bath on the
second floor rent free, and of course access to the whole house. I was
very appreciative of that. Mom was low key to live with---other than
when she broke out singing an opera aria or some Celine Dion song.
I paid for all my food, car expenses, did most of my own cooking,
and Mom picked up my health insurance for me.

# Chapter 13

## The Daily Grind

One time after boating the Little White Salmon, having dinner, and watching some video, I decided it was time to head back home. It was already midnight, and I faced a six-hour drive ahead of me. About six in the morning, I cruised towards the little town of Caldwell, Idaho, still 30 minutes away from the house. It had been a long drive and I was ready for bed. Being a Monday morning, rush hour traffic increased the closer I got to home. I realized these people were just beginning their day, heading towards their daily grind. What a bummer it must be to have to be at work at 7:00 in the morning, five days a week, year 'round.

This was just another reminder of how great my life was. For the past six hours while all these folks were sleeping, I was driving home. I wanted to get home and get up by 11:00 a.m. to take my pictures to be developed so I could boat again. I wondered if the people rushing to work in a haze, knew how I lived my life, would they get angry that I have it so easy, or would they be happy for me and wish me luck?

My life is the way it is because of the decisions I've made in the past. Everybody has the choice of what to do with their own lives, but it seems as if some people don't realize it. Any one of those tired looking people could do exactly what I do: eat, sleep, and kayak. I was happy a lot of them didn't, but it was possible.

Sure I lived in my car, didn't make much money, and didn't get to shower often, but I wouldn't have had it any other way. Traveling all over the country, enjoying life to its fullest, I saw tons of beautiful rivers, met lots of new people, and ate out a lot. I don't know why all these "grinders" didn't do it too. You only live once, so live it.

# Chapter 14

## Creeking and First Descents: Lessons Learned

Skip came from Colorado for the Boise County Throwdown Rodeo at Climax wave on the Payette. It was his first visit to Idaho. Later he spent a couple summers working with Cascade Raft and Kayak Company near Horseshoe Bend, Idaho. Skip stayed at our townhouse. Over the years several other kayakers stayed with Mom and me including Jay Moffatt, Corey Boux, Nikki Kelly, and others. Mom said it was always a pleasure; she really enjoyed the kayak crowd.

"Why don't we take Skip up the Middle Fork of the Payette to show him the steeps for lunch?" I asked Dan who had just gotten back from California. Dan was in. He said, "Also there's a creek up there that I remember wanting to check out." We really are spoiled in Idaho, often being able to have a wilderness kayaking experience with very little travel, right in our own backyard so to speak.

The Middle Fork drainage was geologically unique for the area, containing nice granite bedrock, so we assumed the creeks that fed it would also have that same geology. We drove to the confluence of the creek and hiked up far enough to wet our appetites, which wasn't very far at all. Just seeing the bottom, which looked like a perfect flow and size for the creek, got our adrenaline glands racing. Pulling out the maps we spotted a road that crossed the creek about five miles upstream. We were pumped since Skip had a nice four-wheel drive vehicle, and we usually didn't have access to 4WD's. He was excited as well because he had never been to Idaho, let alone way back in the boonies.

When we arrived at the put-in, Dan and I got even more pumped. Impressive granite mountains surrounded a huge meadow. Silver Creek was still plenty big, and we had come up quite a bit in elevation. The creek was flat for more than a mile at this point as well, meaning the gradient would be more centralized. Dan and I discussed the reasons we shouldn't do the run that day. We only had our playboats since we were there for the next day's rodeo, and it was getting late. After 15 minutes debating and weighing our options we started suiting up. Circumstances were too good to let this opportunity pass. We most likely wouldn't be able to get back here with our own vehicles. Skip was willing to shuttle for us, and the water had been coming down pretty fast recently. It was a go.

Before the put-in Dan and I advised Skip to camp out if he didn't see us by dark, and hopefully we'd see him in the morning. We knew we had to make this exploratory run as quickly and safely as possible. Before we put-in, a fisherman wandered over and offered his sage advice, "You boys are going to break them little boats if you go down there." We thanked him as we put-in. The flat section seemed to be longer than we had thought; plus there were numerous downed trees that we had to sneak under, portage around, or crawl over. We were both getting a little sketched with the amount of wood that was starting to appear in the water.

Finally we came up to the start of the gradient. Amongst the rapids were logs and logjams. We did the first couple of Class IV drops, then had to portage three more rapids clogged with wood. This wasn't a good sign. We had barely gone two miles and already portaged six times due to wood--- typical Idaho creeking. As we went in deeper and deeper the logjams came more steadily.

Starting to worry about daylight, we saw a beautiful granite gorge, an amazing feature rarely found in Idaho. Both our jaws dropped. This was not going to be good with the amount of sunlight left and the wood. We proceeded to scout which revealed that the entrance to the gorge was an unrunnable slot with a log in it. Continuing to scout the gorge we spotted another huge logjam further down. We would have to accomplish this hellacious portage as fast as possible because of the setting sun. Climbing up the mountain, we side-hilled over about a quarter mile, then slowly traversed down after the gorge opened back up.

Finally back in our boats the pace began to pick up. We noticed the wood had diminished dramatically since the gorge. We paddled small rapids without having to portage. Then we arrived at a much larger horizon line. Looking at each other and smiling, we got out of our boats to check it out.

Having found an awesome Class V double drop without wood, we were psyched. Deciding I'd run it first, I drew closer in my boat recalling the line in my head. Left stroke off the first lip, land on a right stroke in a slot no wider than a paddle and a half in turbulent water, then give a quick, hard left boof stroke off the second ledge clearing the hydraulic at the bottom. I felt like the first kayaker ever to take on the challenge of this awesome rapid. I also knew there was no room for a mistake because of the daylight situation, which was getting quite bad since we didn't know how far the takeout was. I hit my line perfectly and whooped for joy at the bottom, waiting for Dan. Dan followed not far behind and went deep off both ledges with a sketchy line, but all was good.

We proceeded with lightning speed finding several more rapids and even slides--- uncommon in Idaho. There was very little wood by this point which really improved our outlook on not having to camp there. This was good, especially since we didn't have sleeping bags. The rapids started to smooth out and the water took on a swift nature. We encountered only two more logs, one requiring portage and the other requiring the boat limbo. Daylight faded to the point where the wood was almost invisible, and we were both thinking about camping when we saw the bridge at the takeout. Yells and more whoops of joy abounded. All was good and the plan had turned out perfectly.

Now we had just enough time to go to the rodeo party which had already started and kick back some beers to make it a little harder to compete tomorrow---just another day in the life of---me.

*\*\*\**

When first descenting you never know if the creek you're interested in will be paddleable, let alone good. It's hit or miss in this ball game. In the early part of spring 2000, before the water started flowing, Dan, Andrew and I were charging through the brush every weekend trying to find new quality creeks in Idaho and Oregon. We scouted up to ten creeks in a weekend. If even one of these turned out to be big enough with not too much wood, it was written down on our list of upcoming kayaking adventures. After scouting many different drainages, creeks, and streams, we knew we had found enough to keep us busy. It was looking to be an adventurous season.

As the weather starts heating up in Idaho, the snowmelt kicks off. Accordingly, the first descent on our list was a low elevation, very small, very steep creek. Upon quick examination of our maps, Little Squaw Creek in eastern Idaho looked like a steep, 400+ feet per mile. This is a lot in Idaho because we don't have waterfalls of a pool drop nature very often. What really drew us to this creek was the fact that much of the drainage was well below the tree line so we didn't think logs would be a problem. Our good buddy Matthew Elam joined Dan and me for our first exploratory trip of that year.

At the put-in the creek was looking perfect; big enough to paddle but not too much water. Once we arrived in the canyon, the creek took on a different feel than the one I had dreamed of the night before. For six miles we mostly hiked with our boats across steep, rocky slopes high above the creek, which plummeted down, down, down. It never stopped; just one long rapid with random wood and brush everywhere. In a couple of places we had to get in and make a sketchy move to the other side so we could continue portaging. Much of it could have been paddleable by itself but the miles of seamless, unrunnable whitewater was disappointing.

Luckily we arrived at a smaller, relatively flat section that we got to paddle. This portion lasted about a mile in the middle of the creek, and was some of the scariest Class III/IV that we'd ever experienced. Brush was the key word here. Under brush, brush jams, and brush so thick that scouting was not an option. After a grueling day of hiking six of the seven miles and worrying about a possible bivouac, we finally reached a road. When I got home that night and looked at the topo map again, I found out we had read the gradient lines wrong and that the creek was 800 feet per mile, not the 400 we thought it was. Lesson learned: look at maps very closely and scout more than a mile of the river ahead of time.

\*\*\*

Rodeos are a staple of kayaking itineraries. Between 1999 and 2002, I competed in over 30 rodeos in Idaho, Oregon, Washington, Montana, Wyoming, and California. The main events were freestyle and down river racing. My favorite was freestyle. A cash prize provided inspiration. My rankings varied. At the 2000 Boise County Throwdown, 2001 Canyon Creek Race, and Jackson Hole I placed first. I placed 2nd at Wenatchee and at the Boise County Throwdown in 2002. That year I was ranked 20th in a field of 64 in the Men's K1 Pro. My friends Dan Menten, Dru West, Matt Elam, Brett Gleason, Corey Boux, Tyko Isaacson, and Tao Berman, all placed very well at these events.

A good rodeo ends with a rockin' party in the evening. Free beer and free food fueled a high energy crowd. Free massages eased our aching shoulders and backs. The rivers glowed with flood lights and disco balls. These parties always included loud, fast music and dancing, sometimes with live bands. Mechanical bull rides , and even mud wrestling added to the festivities. Teva hosted one of the best parties. They provided a 25-foot ramp that shot kayakers 10 feet through the air and into the lake. Boaters were huckin' huge off the ramp going for donkey flips, doubles, donkeys with 180s, pinwheels and inverts.

In early spring 2000, Dan and I headed out on the Rodeo circuit starting with the Kernville Rodeo, followed by the Trinity Rodeo (both of them in California) and then the Oregon Cup, which consisted of Bob's Hole, and the Maupin Days Festival on the

Deschutes River. We also went to Pacific City on the Oregon coast. Six of us stayed in one motel room where we burned a hole in the carpet cooking on a camp stove.

Dan and I decided to boat the Kaweah River in California. We arrived at Hospital Rock in the afternoon and decided we didn't have enough time to boat that section. Farther up the road we saw Marble Creek, which looked like fun. We hiked a couple of miles up a trail to access the creek. This put us high above the river. It was starting to get dark. We came upon a steep cliff slab and had to drop into a gully. Dan got into some poison ivy, but somehow I was spared. We powered through incredibly thick manzanitas and chaparral bushes that poked our skin and tore up our gear.

We had to throw our boats beyond each section of brush, crawl underneath the bushes, and repeat the process all over again. After an hour of this we were both hot and tired. When we finally got to the creek we decided to portage some beautiful drops. A year later, we would have the skill and confidence to boat those same drops, but we were rightfully cautious that day. One of the drops we portaged was a 50-foot sliding falls that corkscrewed off the rock bottom and shot towards the cliff wall. It was unlike anything we'd ever seen. We ended up with some clean runs and had a good time.

***

On the way home from our month long road trip to Cali and Oregon, Dan and I discussed what creeks and rivers we could boat during the rest of the season. We weren't about to let our experience on Little Squaw Creek hinder our ambitions, although it significantly shortened our list of possible first descents. We had been doing a lot of creek boating in the last month and were ready for more. We talked of some first descents that we had scouted out earlier in the spring. One in particular kept jumping out at us whenever our conversation led to first descents--- the Middle Fork of the Weiser River.

Having scouted the bottom two miles of this five mile run, we knew this section would have some good Class V rapids in it and would be worth the drive. The three miles we had not scouted looked very promising on the topo maps: 370 feet per mile in a very steep canyon. The lower section that we had already scouted was 270 feet per mile and looked like tons of fun. We double-checked to make sure we were reading correctly this time.

Ambitions were high, and we were psyched. Dan, Andrew and I headed out May 14 for the Middle Fork of the Weiser. The plan was to at least boat the stuff we had already seen and scout the canyon we had not seen. On the way up the water level looked really inviting. It was a bit low but helped to calm the nerves because this meant there would be more eddies. The rapids we had seen before looked awesome with only one new log that didn't look like a problem. We drove up the switchbacks towards the put-in and decided to hike down into the canyon to determine the runnability of the upper section. What we could see looked like a lot of fun--- a pool drop and Class IV+ boating with no logs. It was a go! Driving the rest of the windy road, we reached a point close enough to the creek to put in.

Once on the river, we took to our usual first descent routine of slow eddy hopping. We portaged one logjam in the flat section before the canyon began. Being from Idaho this was second nature to us. We expected to see many more log jams throughout the day. The rapids picked up with some ledges and boulder gardens. Every piece of wood we came to was manageable, whether it meant limbo-ing under it or just scooting around it. There were even two drops made by wood underneath the water, which created ledges for us.

I noticed the canyon walls starting to get lower and lower, which I figured meant we were nearing the end of this section when we came up to our biggest horizon line yet. Dru hopped out of his boat because it was his turn to scout and video. He started whooping and yelling at us to come and scout too. He was all amped up about whatever he was looking at. I got out and ran up to the lip of the drop. I hadn't seen a waterfall this beautiful for awhile, especially in Idaho. It was not your average clean waterfall. The question was, would this drop be runnable? It was completely free of logs and debris, however.

It had an easy four-foot boof entrance move, a three-stroke pool, then a 12-footer landing on a rock shelf, then sliding off eight feet into a gnarly hole. Dru and I contemplated whether it was runnable. Would we break our boats or worse, our backs? It was hard to tell. What would other sensible kayakers do in this situation? Easy: throw in a big log and see if it shatters into a million pieces. Dan and Dru found a good-sized log and heaved it in.

It looked to us like the log had a pretty smooth line so Dru stepped forward and said he was going for it. With all his ambition and eagerness neither Dan nor I were going to step in his way. I grabbed my rope and Dan grabbed the video camera and we got set up.

Left stroke, right stroke, left, right boof off the first ledge---clean. Left, right, left, hard off the lip, lean forward---bam, take the hit on the ledge off the eight-footer. Dru was at the bottom, right side up and still paddling! He looked a little dazed but not too bad. Hollers rang out from Dan and me. "How was it? How much did it hurt?"

"It was sweet! Didn't hurt too bad."

"Right on. I'm going!" I yelled.

Heading back up to my boat, my heart pumped harder than it had for quite some time. I could feel nature's drug adrenaline caressing my mind and body. I hopped in my boat, waited for the thumbs up, and was on my way. First ledge---no problem, quick strokes, boof hard, land at 45 degrees, left stroke through the hole. "Yeeaaa!" I yelled out. I was amazed that I barely felt the hit. A 12-footer onto a rock shelf had to hurt more than that, right? After the lead in the creek immediately dropped another eight feet. I threw my fist up in the air.

Dan was next and took the hardest hit of all. He swore he wouldn't run it again, but we would wait and see if he changed his mind next year. We decided to name it "King Kong Falls" because King Kong was a big mean sucker but had a sweet heart inside, just like this drop. In fact this falls was worth the whole run itself.

We came up to the longest and ugliest rapid of the day. This one consisted of a small ledge with a log paralleling it at the entrance, a steep and tight little S-turn move in the middle, then a seven-foot ledge at the bottom with a log angling off of it to the left. I scouted it quickly and decided I was going first. I hit the first move clean and was lining up for the S-turn move when I hit a rock that I had not expected to be a problem. Bam! I pitoned hard into it sending me all the way across the current against a rock with a small log sticking out of it. Log to the face. Oww! Through the S-turn upside down, rolled up quickly and made the last move, no time to worry. I rolled up two strokes before the last ledge. Damn, not one of my cleaner lines, but I was okay at the bottom. "Oh well," I thought, "we needed some good crash and burn video this year anyway."

Dru was up next and had a bit cleaner line but not by much. The next section was an easy roadside scout and gnarly. After seeing two ugly lines on this nasty rapid, Dan decided it should be called "Helter Skelter" and decided it wasn't the day for running it himself.

Only one easy rapid left and we were at the takeout. What a day it had been. No rapid portages, some fun rapids, a gnarly rapid, and a breathtaking waterfall. This creek turned out to be one of the best creeks I had paddled in Idaho, and the closest to Boise. We were psyched; this was a day we would remember.

We didn't let our encounter with a grizzled looking fisherman dampen our spirits. Still setting up camp after a day's fishing, he looked warily at us as we carried our boats past him and finally asked if we had just come down *that* canyon. When we said yes, he shook his head and said, "Can't nobody go down that canyon and live!" We chuckled softly as we left him.

***

"Damn dude, what time did we go to bed?" I asked Dru. As with many other kayaking mornings, this one had that certain alcohol stinging ring to it. You know, the one that bites at your whole body.

"Dude, I need some food. I don't know about first descentin' today, damn," I moaned. But we had been planning on this for quite some time now. We weren't going to let a little partying get in our way. So we quickly chowed down, grabbed the cameras and headed out.

Dan, Dru, and I had met Tyko Isaacson at a recent Rodeo tour. He was from La Grande, Oregon. Tyko was fighting fires in uncharted and off the beaten path areas in the mountains east of La Grande. He filled us in on a little secret--- a set of mountains unexplored by boaters full of sick paddling---the Eagle Cap Wilderness area in the Wallowa mountain range. Tyko was friends with Tao Berman, who he knew would paddle the gorge, but Tyko only wanted to share this first descent with his crew of peers, rather than let Tao continue to get all the glory. After hearing that from Tyko, we decided it had to be top quality and the plans were made.

The four of us set out on June 11, 2000 to conquer Hurricane Creek in Cannibal Gorge. After getting off the highway, we drove farther and farther into the unknown. Around this time, serious kayakers had to search way off the beaten path for first descents. We had heard that three miles into this roadless area there was a short creek in a gorge that was simply incredible.

As we approached the entrance to the wilderness, the after effects of my drinking from the night before started to wear off. We reminisced about kayaking glory days, girls, and parties as we often did. Dru told us he was really feeling good that day and was in the groove. I knew how good it was for a boater when the water was sick and they were in the groove. I, on the other hand, was not quite up to par although still stoked.

On the way up Tyko talked about how the creek looked like it was around the same level as when he had scouted it and that the gorge was going to be awesome. Waterfalls, slides, good rapids, no logs, all in a sheer walled gorge. When we got to the trailhead Tyko informed us that he had brought some deer packing pack-frames and that we could strap our kayaks to them to make the hike much easier. Unfortunately he only had three so Dru generously offered to carry his boat on his shoulders. We got half-dressed, readied the cars for departure and strapped our boats to our backs. We looked ahead at the trail for a moment, eagerly anticipating the day.

We set out on a three-mile hike to the gorge. Every step we took was that much further into this beautiful hidden wilderness area. The creek below us however, was pure mank, full of wood, and looked like trash. This made us wonder, but when we arrived the gorge was awesome, as promised. Because the rock in this area was limestone, this gorge had a reoccurring theme to it: undercuts. The entire right side was slowly wearing away creating caves, undercuts, and overhanging walls the whole way down. The upper rapid consisted of boulder-garden-sliding drops, tiny slot-falls with caves in them, and the crux of a left sliding waterfall against an undercut wall the whole way down. There were no pools in this upper part of the gorge and no room for a mistake. It was definitely the most committing stretch of whitewater we had ever contemplated running. You had to be on top of your game to run this.

The lower section simply looked like good tough fun. An 18-footer, an S-turn to 10-footer, and a really tight and fun looking S-turn rapid. As I scouted further up the gorge the rapids grew in difficulty. My jaw dropped. This upper section looked burly. Tyko was amazed at how much more water there was in the gorge than when he had scouted it. Apparently when he had scouted it there were pools in between all the upper drops. He guessed that there was almost two to three times the amount of water now than when he had last seen it. The upper gorge had changed from good Class V to fringe V+/VI.

The run from the top started off with a 30-foot slide put-in from a subsidiary creek. From that point on, it was a nonstop string of walled in drops, and you were committed. The first drop wasn't much of a concern. It led into a steep rocky rapid that turned to the left with a boulder just barely to the right of the exit move. A few quick strokes through another steep rapid led to a really narrow semi waterfall/slide type of thing with a nasty piton rock pointing up stream on the right creating a small cave. Immediately after this was the crux of the whole gorge, an abrupt pile turning to the right then onto a 10-foot slide going back to the left with the right wall totally overhanging and the pool below all undercut. If you made it here you had made it to the lower fun stretch. It looked nerve-wracking.

Dan, Tyko, and I decided that the upper gorge was dedicated to the right person on the right day. We could see the line but could not see ourselves on that line that day. We were not going home empty handed, however. We decided that our move would be to rappel into the pool below the crux move and put-in there. We were just starting to hook up the rappel line when Dru finally arrived. He was beat; the hike had been hell for him. When he saw the gorge his eyes started lighting up. He started scampering all over, scouting out the gorge.

From a distance it looked like he was planning to run it. We discussed it with him and we were right. He was going to run the entire gorge. At this point his face turned from excitement to sheer focus. We hatched a plan to paddle in twosomes so we could video one another from the gorge rim. Dan would rappel down to the pool after the crux drop to the put in and set safety. Tyko would also set up as close as he could to the crux move with a rope. And I would be on video duty.

We started suiting up and getting ready. Nervous for Dru, we were still stoked that he felt like he could paddle this amazing rapid. If he succeeded in paddling this rapid it would be the toughest thing he had ever paddled. We set up safety and cameras. Dan rappelled down and we roped his boat down to him. Tyko got set up, and I found a good vantage point for filming. It took us a long time to get ready. Dru waited patiently in his boat the whole time. Finally the yell rang out, and I gave the thumbs up signal.

When Dru dropped in I know my heart stopped for the forty-five seconds of non-stop paddling that he did to make it to the eddy where Dan waited. First rapid, no worries. Next rapid with the rock at the bottom, little back ender but all good. He pushed on. Through the viewfinder Dru looked solid, cleaning the next couple of rapids and still paddling strong. Up to the tight drop with the cave half way down, he shot through it with tons of speed and emerged paddling hard for the corkscrewing pillow crux move. He busted around the pillow and made the left turn onto the slide.

"Crack!" It must have echoed across the entire wilderness area when Dru's paddle hit the overhanging wall. He slid on his face and elbow down the slide crux. When he hit the pool at the bottom where Dan was, his boat quickly floated to the left away from the undercut and he rolled up. Yells went out from all of us except him. Forty-five seconds of continuous, solid paddling and there he was at the bottom. From my viewfinder he looked a little dazed. Dan held his boat there in the eddy because he was so high on adrenaline he could hardly talk, smile, or anything.

Finally Dan got in his boat and they headed down the rest of the run. The 18- footer was awesome; S-turn to 10-footer with a cave on the right, sweet. Tight S-turn with cave, excellent. They were both at the bottom and had the biggest smiles on their faces I had ever seen. We went down and talked to them about the run and their feelings and anything else that spewed out of our rambling mouths.

Tyko and I started suiting up and preparing to run it at a mile a minute. We were so pumped to get in our boats. Now it was our turn to rappel into the gorge and "have at" the lower section. I roped my boat down first to create tension on the line for when I rappelled down. Just roping into this gorge was adrenalizing. When I reached the bottom I got in my boat, paddled the 18-footer cleanly, got out in the pool below and waited for Tyko.

The put-in was not the place to wait. Rocks tumbled down all the time coming inches from you and your boat. You had to take cover under a tiny overhanging ledge hoping not to get clocked. Tyko rappelled in first and then began the stressful wait for his boat. Every time I heard Dru yell, "Rock!" I would relay the message to Tyko and cringe. It was the scariest thing just watching; I can't even imagine how Tyko felt. I saw huge rocks plunge down the steep wall, barely missing Tyko and sending out a huge splash.

Finally Tyko was in his boat and we headed down the creek. Everything went well. When we got out it was starting to get pretty dark. We grabbed our gear and made our way back to the trail towards the car. The last quarter mile of our hike was in the dark, but we finally got there. We were all tired and worn out, but exhilarated. We had found an amazing creek with incredible rapids and a beautiful gorge--- and we safely conquered it. We made sure when we got back there was time to rally with the La Grande chicks.

***

There was one other creek we had to hit in the Wallowa Mountains before the water was gone. This was a great find in eastern Oregon for Andrew, Tyko, and myself. We set out on August 6, 2000 to run it. This creek had an awesome three-tiered waterfall, but it also had a short gorge above. The problem with the waterfall was that it had a big log blocking the entrance. On our previous trip to Hurricane Creek we had scouted the West Wallowa and tried to move the log on several occasions; but this time Tyko had rounded up the correct equipment to make this run a reality. Using a throw rope, 4,000 pound webbing, and a big come-along, the log was finally in a place where we could run the falls. Unfortunately it swayed above our first move, suspended still by our rigged up come-along. We didn't want to let it go though, for fear of it floating back into a position that would make the drop unrunnable again.

Sanitarium Falls consisted of a left boof to get around the suspended log, and a big boil at the lip of a nice 30-foot vertical falls landing in a pool with logs floating in an undercut cave, then a sweet 15-foot seam drop. Watching Tyko style this drop was worth the whole day. All in all it was an awesome run. This had definitely been a good season finding several new quality creeks and filming all of them. All of these were soon to appear in our video *The Revolution.*

# Chapter 15

## Beware of "Hype"

When I'm kayaking, I feel the adrenaline pumping every time we round a blind corner. "Don't go river left here, someone broke their boat there, so and so got worked hard here, huge holes at this other place." Often this is all I could think of because people had told me so many different stories. Every rapid got less intimidating though. I started to wonder. All those stories I had heard about this rapid must be in here somewhere, and we were almost done with the run. Anticipating what we had heard, each corner was more exciting--- then bam!

"Sweet, we made it! What did you think?"

"What do you mean we made it? Where were the huge holes? The place where Billy Bob broke his arm? The rapid with four 'must make moves' before the mandatory portage? We didn't even portage!"

Hype: we've all heard it and all of us get sick of it. Every adrenaline hungry, water lovin' one of us has heard it and been disappointed about a run because of it. "Flavor Flave" put it best when he said "Yaaaaa booeeeey!! Don't believe the hype!"

It can happen to runs of all difficulties, sizes, and shapes. There are a few things that help create the hype and a few things you can do to weed your way through it. First, what are some of the things that create the hype? If the hype only appears in local guidebooks, look at the publishing date and the type of boats in the pictures. This run might have been cutting edge back in the fiberglass days, but maybe not in the days of a 98-foot waterfall.

Next, if the hype comes from numerous sources far and wide, consider the type of people telling the story. Every time you hear another tale about the same run, think: is this the type of boater who would end up taking a swim in your favorite play hole and have an experience with God? Or is this the local video star who if he gets worked by the river, you don't want any part of that? Also, look at your surroundings and the type of boaters who regularly visit this area. Are there only class III rivers within four hours of this creek? Or is it all "nar" as far as a tank of gas will get you? Are these the type of boaters you would want to boat with or the type of people you'd just be satisfied drinking a beer with?

Locals are the kings of creating and compounding hype. There are many reasons for this. For instance, they don't want outsiders messing up their awesome runs, or the first descent ten years ago went badly and nobody is willing to go back. Locals are notorious for taking an old folklore legend as fact and not questioning it. Ten years in the rumor mill with the same exaggerated story does a lot to that story.

Do your own research about the river. Take all the stories you've heard about a run, evaluate the sources of them, look at a topo map, and try to find actual pictures or video of the run, and consider the exaggeration factor. Find someone who has run it within the last couple of weeks. Also consider the flow level. Were these stories involving today's water level or are these flood-stage horror stories? Water level plays a big factor in hype; for example, that stretch you just ran in 30 minutes is listed in the guidebook as a half day Class IV that will leave the boater grateful to be alive and off the river.

Hype will always continue as long as we boat, so weed your way through it and choose your runs wisely. Make up your own mind.

# Chapter 16

## West Virginia with Andrew West

I had such a great time with Jordan in West Virginia the previous year that I was stoked to go again, this time with Dru. We set off early September 2000, shortly after the Salt Lake City Trade Show, in Dru's red Benz with $600 and the hope of an extended season on the Gauley. The Benz was loaded with our kayaks on the top rack. We filmed throughout our adventure.

West Virginia had awesome kayaking by day, but at night there wasn't a lot to do. Nevertheless, Dru and I had a lot of fun. I only scored two days of video boating since it was a bit late in the season for me to land this job again.

While in West Virginia we got used to the accent and enjoyed putting on the accent ourselves. We interviewed people in front of the local Walmart, showing them magazines and photos of extreme kayakers. We asked what they thought of the sport, and if they liked the kayakers that came in the summer. Most of them seemed a little leery of us. Perhaps we looked a bit unkempt and sketchy.

We often picked up an elderly hitchhiker, a mentally challenged man who called himself "The General." We enjoyed listening to him regale us with stories of his life, even though he was a bit difficult to understand. He always appreciated the ride.

One time we decided to take an airplane ride in a four-seat Cessna. We wanted to enjoy a bird's eye view of the beautiful rivers meandering through the lush rolling hills of West Virginia. An elderly gentleman slowly hobbled out onto the airstrip with the assistance of a walker. We thought, "What the heck is that man doing on the runway?" He slowly approached our plane, and then got in. We found out why the ride was only five dollars apiece---this elderly man who used a walker was our pilot! We were a bit nervous, but the scenery was beautiful and we made it back in one piece.

Our trip lasted five weeks and included kayaking in beautiful upstate New York and Montreal on the St. Lawrence River in Quebec as well. The St. Lawrence is so big we had to paddle about half a mile or more to get to the waves.

Montreal is the "stripper capital" of Canada. It was cool that we didn't have to be 21 in Canada to enjoy the scene. And the pizza in Montreal was awesome. Everywhere we went they served big slices for a great price, which was fortunate because we had very little money left to last the 3000 miles remaining to get home. As usual, broke through most of the trip, we continued our diet of Ramen, heat-gun-heated pizza, and leftovers from raft trips and buffets. At a buffet such as Chuck-A-Rama, we loaded our plates, surreptitiously packing lots of food into plastic containers hidden in our backpacks.

We stopped off in the mornings at various hotels to avail ourselves of their free breakfasts, even though we hadn't slept at their establishment. One time a staff person came up and asked, "Are you two guests here?" We said, "Yes." She asked, "What room are you in?" Dru said, "Room 325." She said, "We don't have three floors," and sent us on our way. We weren't proud of these escapades, but we had to eat.

After almost two months of losing boats from the car, camping in industrial areas, waking up to the car spinning out of control at 70 mph due to total exhaustion and falling asleep at the wheel, a nearly busted tire, and 42 hours of straight driving, we were home in time for the snow to fall. We literally drove into Boise with about one dollar between us.

When we got back the North Fork of the Payette was up a bit. So the last day of the season was spent dropping Jacob's Ladder and the rest of the middle five miles on a day that was 40 degrees, with snow on the ground. It was awesome. That last day was also my 105th time on the river for this season, and a damn good one it was. All in all, my first year dedicating my life to try to make a career in kayaking had been very productive. I felt my boating level, skill, form, and mindset had increased dramatically. For the first time I realized I paddled at a professional level.

The addiction ran deep and our pockets weren't as deep, unfortunately. Andrew and I really put our noses to the grindstone when winter came along. Dru landed three jobs and about killed himself with work. I plugged into long, cold, lonesome day and night double shifts at the local ski resort.

I was working on a ten-minute video for an Outdoor Life Network (OLN) contest. I sold some of this footie to OLN in 2003. I had just bought video editing capturing software/hardware for my computer so my nights were filled staring at the bright screen, seeing the same captions over and over, and basically burning my retinas out. Operating on a shoe string budget, Dru and I were working on a little "zine" and interviewing people for it. I also took a lot of still photos that winter to learn more about photography. I skateboarded at least three times a week to keep in shape.

# Chapter 17

### Kill the Boise Bore!

Our souls were ripped out the day the weather turned cold and Idaho's rivers dried up to evil, Old Man Winter. Every winter Dru and I chomped at the bit, impatient to get back to kayaking by early spring or sooner. We wracked our brains to come up with something fun and interesting to do and came up with "urban kayaking." You might have seen it on Outdoor Life Network, Fox Television, or MTV and thought of it as just some California get-rich-quick-scheme. But no, it started in Boise, Idaho with two young, broke kids, counting the days till the return of their souls---the first sign of melting water.

Dru and I created urban kayaking not only because of deprivation, but also because of our love of kayaking and the need for fun at all costs throughout the cold, stagnant Boise winters. You too can experience thrills your momma never knew.

It all started when we ran out of money at the end of summer. Dan, Dru, our friend Dustin Urizar, and later Graham Wright started out hurtling down the foothills near Boise in our kayaks. Unfortunately there was no carnage to be had. This sparked an idea about trying other things. Not wanting to stop the day-to-day routine of kayaking, we took to the streets to put our whitewater skills to the concrete test. Starting with sliding down mountainsides and stairs, we quickly progressed to flinging ourselves off rooftops, buildings, and concrete drops. So how does a beginner get involved in this diversionary sport?

First, start with the basics. I assume you have a kayak. Next, you need to get comfortable on concrete. Sliding down a mountainside can be fun, although dirt can be really sticky, which makes for a slow, boring ride. The more obstacles you have to contend with, like bushes, trees, people, and cars in streets, the more entertaining the session will be.

Stairs are quite two-faced. Some are really slow and mellow whereas others are super-fast and fun. Be forewarned, when hitting stairs for the first time, the material the stairs are made of makes a huge difference. As a general rule, concrete is very rough so it is the slowest to slide on, whereas metal is super slick and fast for a boat. Also, kinks in stairs and what lies below them come into play. Sometimes a set of bushes at the bottom is a good way to stop. Depending on where they lie and the number of steps, a kink in a set of stairs usually provides great air. Take note though that concrete is much harder than water to land on. Other times you may have to slide out into the street and deal with traffic. After you get comfortable with concrete, speeds, and the general feel of urban kayaking, you are ready to take it to the next level.

The next level is determined by your fear factor; if you have plenty of ego and machismo you will continue to pursue urban kayaking. Your knowledge of how your boat and body react as a single entity and your imagination are all you need. Truthfully you can try whatever you think is possible.

Next you will want to go bigger and catch more air. You'll need something to cushion the blow and something to lessen the angle of your fall. To cushion the blow, you'll need some sort of a crash pad--- a mattress is big enough to allow a little room for error and soft enough to land on from a substantial height. To lessen the angle of the fall you need some sort of a landing plank. Anything you can land and slide on while on the way to your crash pad will do. The length and width of the landing plank is determined by how much room for error you want and your access to materials to construct it with.

Don't forget that the same laws about speed and material mentioned in "the basics" also apply here. If you make a 25-foot long metal landing plank, your speed will greatly increase once you make contact with it. It's also a good idea to have several landing planks. Landing planks can be stacked on top of each other to keep decreasing the angle of the original plank. To pull off a multi-tiered section, you will need more than one landing plank.

Something else that will really help you perform at that next level is a companion---a good friend who knows you well and is willing to help you on your quest to become a better, more well-rounded person. Somebody to laugh, cry, hide, and hurry with. With urban kayaking these ingredients are necessities to start boating off rooftops and buildings.

Usually roofs lack a nice flat spot where you can get in your boat and prepare to launch. Your friend needs to help you get your boat up, hold it steady while you get in, and if you can't hold on to anything, your friend must hold you until you're ready to go. Urban kayaking is like whitewater boating; you never want to do it alone. This is an important safety issue. If you miss your line or incorrectly calculate what you thought would happen, you're going to need a friend to take you to the hospital.

Dru and I also devised a boat launch. The idea came from driving to a kayak destination with the boats strapped on top of the car. We worried that the straps weren't tight enough. We imagined the boat flying through the air at Mach 2. We called Dustin to try a new move using his car in the experiment. He was in.

We decided the new freeway under construction would be a good place to catch some air. Dustin was pumped and said that he wanted to try getting some 180s and 360s in the dirt as well. I was pumped because I would be on the sidelines filming. And Dru was pumped because he would get to see an awesome spectacle. When we got there we removed the straps holding the kayak to the roof of the car and told Dustin to gun it. When he got to the dirt, he slammed the brakes and the boat shot into the horizon.

None of us could contain ourselves. It was one of the funniest things we'd seen done with a boat. We put it back on the racks and rallied several more times, busting spins and even trying a little bowling with the construction cones. Quality entertainment.

Dru and I discovered what it takes when we began to use concrete as a playground. Urban kayaking debuted in our video *The Revolution*. In addition, I put together a small video highlighting urban kayaking antics which I sold to Fox Network's sports show, *You Gotta See This*. It aired several times. After reading this or having seen *The Revolution*, if you think you have what it takes to be an urban kayaker, you may just want to grab a kayak and head into the streets of your hometown.

Dru knew some friends who owned a speedboat, and when winter ended they invited us to tag along one day to Lucky Peak Reservoir northeast of Boise. Although this didn't quite fit the description of urban kayaking, it was a lot of fun. We tied our kayaks behind their boat and enjoyed several trips around the lake, catching waves, and doing tricks. These antics were later included in our *Revolution* video as well.

Dru and I also had fun in the warm months with boogie boarding. This sport consists of tying a rope to a 3x3-foot board and attaching it to a tree on the bank of the river. We attached two ropes to the board and wrapped these around our wrists for support and control. We got quite adept at surfing a wave, doing underwater flips on the board, and trying to end upright when we surfaced above water.

Of course I had to get video of this as well. Dru, ever the ham, narrated for the footage as I boarded.

"Here we have David Norell, one of the pioneering fathers of contemporary river boarding. Notice the board is now upside down as he sets up for his new signature move, attempting to do a 180-degree rotation and stay on the board the whole time. If I know David, he will soon be able to land this move."

My dog Jenny really loved being with me around water. She would yelp and bark while I was on the board, eager to give it a try herself; so we let her.

Dru commented, "Here we've got David's dog Jenny on the board with him. Jenny is David's long time faithful companion. She's 10 years old, but you'd never know it by looking at her because she's such a youthful, high energy, playful dog--- very much like David himself. You can see the bond between man and man's best friend out here on the river today. David is very proud of his dog and he has every right to be because most dogs can't boogie board as well as Jenny. Uh oh, it appears now as if Jenny is slipping. Can she hold on?"

It was amazing how well she managed to balance herself on that board.

# Chapter 18

### Still Twitchin'

"All right, sounds good Eric. I'll see you soon." I couldn't believe Eric Link, producer of the *Twitch* series, had just invited me to do some filming for his next video *Still Twitch'n*, along with Tao Berman and Brandon Knapp. Having craved some quality whitewater for awhile now, I knew these guys could provide my fix. I was excited. This would be my first foreign boating experience. I started thinking about whether I had made a wise decision to go along. Being from Idaho, I didn't have tons of waterfall and tough creeking experience under my belt. I had paddled some awesome whitewater around the US but these guys were a step above me. However, I would love to paddle all the creeks featured in the *Twitch* series, so I started packing.

It would be a ten-day trip starting July 10, 2000. I told Mom that I loved her and I'd call when I could, and headed out the door. On the drive to Washington I was apprehensive. I guess you could say I had a "twitchy" feeling. I knew that there seemed to be a general theme in *Twitch 2000* of people getting beat down. But I was so pumped up that I couldn't stand not to paddle and I was confident that my skills were up to par. I just needed to stay completely focused while paddling.

Would this crew be safety conscious? How would they take to me? What about portaging? These questions flew through my head over and over. Two things for sure: I would watch out for my own safety first and foremost, and I would have an awesome time no matter what happened. I was ready…

After postponing the trip a couple of days so Tao could finish some business (which involved running a few waterfalls for a commercial) we were finally on our way. Because there was only one creek containing two runnable drops, we did less paddling on our first day than we would the rest of the trip. We arrived at the creek and Eric descended ahead of us to set up his cameras. When we got down to the drops Tao showed Brandon and me the lines and we climbed in our boats. The drops looked awesome. The first drop was a tight, right-slotted 10-footer against the wall, with the left side being a sieve. It was fun but quite shallow at the lip and hard to set up for. The next drop was a beautiful 40-footer that just barely spat out past vertical.

Considering this had only been the first day with this crew I must say my heart sure did get pumping. After this run we packed up quickly and set out for Canada, eager to get to foreign land. As the night drew near I reflected upon the journey thus far, realizing this was going to be an incredible trip. I couldn't wait for tomorrow.

The second day probably provided us with the best creek I had ever paddled. Although short, the creek was non-stop action from start to finish. The day began with a 4-wheel drive road and our lovely shuttle bunnies swearing they wouldn't drive the cars back. However, they made it and had a fun time doing it. For us though, the day was only beginning. We spent the first hour waiting for Tao and Brandon to finish some business (which involved putting stickers of sponsors on their boats). The next hour or more we bushwhacked our way towards Skookum Creek with no trail, traversing down several cliff bands.

Because this creek was so good, I will only tell about the more outstanding rapids. Once on the creek the action began immediately with a nice 10-foot warm up slide. Next, we came to a 20-footer with a perfect lead-in in for speed. After plenty of good drops we came to one that was completely gorged up. There was no way to portage, no way to escape and hardly a place to scout. It consisted of water bouncing off zigzagging walls, dropping through huge holes, then around a blind corner that could only be scouted/boated once in the rapid. The only option was to boat it so we hopped in and gave it a whirl. I didn't know what might lie around the next corner, or if perchance, *I* might lie around the next corner! It turned out to be a very long, incredible rapid.

The next drop of significance was a perfect 35-footer. It looked very similar to Celestial Falls but slightly smaller. We had heard that another 30-footer still lay ahead of us. At the next big horizon line Brandon hopped out to scout. When he returned all he had to say was, "This isn't a 30-footer!" We ran up to scout for ourselves only to find the most perfect, clean 60-footer. What a treat.

Brandon went first, I second, and Tao lapped it twice for the video. Everyone's adrenaline level was high. Around the next corner we came to a sweet double 25-foot slide and then immediately to the take-out. What a day it had been. We cruised into town to fill our bellies full of some local dank grub before going to sleep.

Canada is a very beautiful place with an amazing amount of continuously flowing water. Canadians are very nice and proud of their country. It was only the third day of the trip and I was psyched to be along. We had a pretty neat change of pace that day, marked by the highest waterfall (by two feet) I'd ever run. Although we still had the vertical walled gorge like the last few days, this creek flowed down the gorge at 3000 cfs. It was simply amazing. The day went by smoothly with some big rapids, big holes, and blazing paddles. In keeping with the trend of this trip, we ended the day with a fatty meal and full stomach.

It had been our first day with the author of Canadian guidebooks and new companion, Stuart Smith. This man had so much knowledge in his cranium.

The more I got to know Stuart, the more I realized how awesome he was. Also the more he got to know us, the more he opened up. When writing his first two guide books he paddled tons of new rivers and creeks all over Canada, many of them solo. He used to slalom race; he had excellent form and was really smooth on the water. I must say that he was one of the best paddlers I've ever met. He was running drops that I portaged, and running them well.

If I had to pick one word that summed up day four of our trip, it would be "stealth." The kayaking extravaganza brought us to a country club/golf course with a beautiful, impressive waterfall-laden gorge directly in the middle of it. Unless we could access the creek from outside the golf course, we would be on private commercial property. For the first part of the morning we found ourselves trying to fit in with the crowd, scouting out the gorge, and dodging security. It must have been quite a sight for the golfers seeing our motley crew cruising around their lovely establishment.

The creek was beautiful with a 10-foot slide at the put-in, a 25-foot-cracked-out falls, a dead vertical 35-footer, a logjam, and finally another 8-footer; all this with the Clubhouse directly above. We were not turning away, not after coming all this way from the States to creek boat. This was prime stomping ground! After scouting we received our plan of action from the high master, Stuart Smith. We knew we would have to transform into top double-0 agents to pull this off. We devised a plan, which we named our "Golf Course Kayaking Mission."

First we had to drive the vehicles to a secluded location so as not to be seen if encountered by local law agents. Next the plan was to get dressed at the cars and place the boats and ourselves in the van. Then we were to casually roll into the parking lot, park in the space closest to the creek, and burst out of the van making a run for the put-in. Not being spotted during this entire operation was our goal.

The first few steps of the plan flew by without error; however when we got to the last step things didn't quite go as planned. About ten yards from the creek we were stopped by security. Damn! They weren't having any part of us in their creek, not with the waterfalls and all--- it was dangerous.

Chatting between Brian, the security guard, and our group went on for about 15 minutes with all of us staring longingly at the put-in. Just about the time we had accepted defeat and started turning around, Tao with his outstanding diplomatic skills was able to persuade the guard into giving us the okay for boating. Our eyes wide with astonishment, we thanked him deeply and ran to the put-in.

One of the concerns Brian had was liability, and I'm sure it didn't help that Stuart slipped and fell ten feet into the river at the put-in. "Are they still watching?" Stuart yelled. Yes, Stuart, they were. The creek itself turned out to be awesome and was the "dry meadow" of British Columbia. Another fantastic day.

Our fifth morning began with delicious banana pancakes again before heading for a roadside creek with only two waterfalls. After paddling the run quickly we drove north to search out a new glorious area. In Canada you don't have to drive very far to find quality boating. After only an hour of driving it was back to good old Canadian bushwhacking to get down to the put-in. Trails and roads seem to be few and far between in Canada.

We boated some restful, splashy, and continuous Class IV that day. What the water lacked in difficulty, was made up for by its beautiful, blue-green color. Stuart informed us the color was due to a glacier less than 20 miles upstream, which drained into the river. Being this close to the glacier of course, the water was burly cold. Outside it must have been 90 degrees yet my hands were completely numb. When we took out we changed and loaded boats as fast as we could because the mosquitoes were horrible. We continued on to our next destination which would be one drainage over.

Waking up on the sixth morning I had a feeling that this was not going to be my best day. First off I simply did not want to get out of bed, a sign that I might be tired throughout the day. I felt like I hadn't slept at all the previous night, even though I had slept well. When I finally did get out of bed the sky was overcast. Our traditional banana pancake breakfast was excellent which helped to liven my mood somewhat.

We were faced with a creek that was flowing moderately at a medium to high flow of 1,000 to 1,200 cfs. I was right about this day not being my best day. On the way to the put-in I slipped, along with my boat, directly into the river. With a holler I scrambled downstream at top speed trying to reach my boat. Once it floated out of sight all I could hope for was that my faithful companions would have it eddied out downstream.

After finally being reunited with my boat I was back in action for another bitter cold but bloody fun creek. The first rapid was a straight forward 18-footer. That day Brandon had a completely different energy level than myself and threw the smoothest freewheel in his creekboat. Everybody's jaw dropped; it was incredible. The rest of the creek consisted of boulder gardens, continuous big water, big holes and a gnarly 40-footer with circulating wood pieces at the bottom. Not being on top of my game I opted for the high and dry line and watched everyone else style their lines.

*\*\**

Kayakers were pushing the limits of what could be done in a kayak, whether it was inventing new moves in a playboat or going off huge waterfalls. The increase in skill level each year was simply amazing. But with the increase in skill level and difficulty of whitewater being run, came the increase in the consequences of missing a line or calculating the outside forces on your boat incorrectly. As the skill level increases it is all the more imperative to carefully assess the risks and potential outcome.

Mamquam Falls in Squamish, BC is a waterfall that seems to play with higher end kayakers like toys. It's in the 60-foot range and looks very clean. With a perfect lead in, huge pool, and easy access, it is the perfect place for video kayakers to get some quality footage; but with the dam upstream, one never knows when the perfect water level will be there.

The Twitch crew had been looking at the waterfall almost every day for a week, waiting for the perfect water level and the ambition to run it. On their last day in town they decided to check it out one more time. Upon arriving they found the place to be swarming with kayakers. The Perception folks filming with Driftwood Productions were nearly suited up and ready to hit it when the Twitch crew arrived. Everyone was still a little antsy about this big drop. Unfortunately, in the rush to get video first, Driftwood sped up their process and got boaters in the water too quickly to get a solid safety system set up. Allen, a professional C1 boater, decided that he was going to be the first to hit this monster, but by no means the first boater to run it. It almost seemed that video was the name of the game and not safety; videographers and their cameras swarmed everywhere.

Once Allen got the signal that the cameras were rolling, he was off. He hit the falls nicely but went so deep we began to worry. His paddle surfaced first so we knew that he wasn't connected to it on the other end. When he came out of his boat he immediately flushed into an undercut cave on the left, out of sight of almost everybody there.

This is when the chaos started; a frenzy of yelling and arm signals began as everybody realized how little had been put into the safety aspect. The general rule for running a waterfall is that the larger the falls, the harder it is to set safety because the safety person on shore is so far away from the boater who is now in a gorge.

After some unsuccessful rope work, it was decided that a boater must get to Allen to make sure he was all right. Tao decided that he could handle this huge waterfall and get to Allen's rescue so he quickly suited up. People flew around. As ropes were being set up and thrown about, Eric ran to a good video spot while Tao scouted frantically. During the chaotic rescue one of the ropers high on the cliff, Todd, slipped and fell into the river without a life vest. Luckily he was okay and got back to shore quickly to continue to help with the rescue.

Grabbing his boat, Tao raced down and was soon in the air cleaning another huge drop as he paddled to Allen's side. Everyone was relieved that Allen would have a resting point now but he still had to be roped out of there quickly. By then he had been in the cold water for nearly 20 minutes. Tao asked to make sure he was still holding on and all Allen could say was, "I'm really tired." After another 20 minutes Allen was sitting on the bank safely; definitely shaken.

The Perception boys had figured out their rescue plan and had worked it down to an easy operation if something else went wrong.

Being men of strong will and great paddling skill, more boaters suited up to conquer this falls.

The next person to hit the falls was Toby. After executing a brief 60-footer surf at the base he was out and into position for his part of the safety. Next up was Dave who boated for Dagger team. The power of the falls ripped his paddle out of his hands but Toby was right there to help him. Still determined to beat this drop, Todd, unscathed by his fall earlier during the rescue, hopped in. Oops, another lost paddle and swimmer. Luckily for him though, their safety was a success this time and he was out in less than two minutes. When they got Todd out they found that he had hit his face on his kayak and split his eyebrow and lip wide open. They immediately called it a day and took him to the nearest hospital, only five minutes away, where he received 12 stitches and a nice scar to help remember the drop.

The Twitcher's decided they had seen enough and wanted to get away from the whole bad vibe that was happening. Since most of our day was gone Stuart mentioned that there was a creek nearby that we might want to run later; we could scout it before heading back to camp. When we arrived we found the first drop was a tight 35-footer with a weird crack rapid below. I didn't scout below this but Brandon said that the creek pumped up the volume and became tight slot after tight, twisting slot with potholes and more cracks. I went to bed that night thinking about what it might look like when we got there. It sounded gnarly; I'd have to stay focused.

Some valuable lessons were learned that day, but the waterfall had not seen the end of its carnage. We heard a few days later the Riot boys rolled into town, stumbled across it and deemed it worthy of excellent footage. The water level looked great. Perhaps their thought was that they could up the ante and throw ends off of it. By the time they finished setting up cameras, dressing and getting their boats to the water's edge, the water had dropped. The dam upstream had stopped releasing and the flow had been cut by nearly half--- a tremendous difference for this waterfall. It had gone from a huge drop with plenty of aeration for cushioning at the bottom, to a huge drop into nearly green water; a solid hit from any height.

After scouting it again it was decided that it was still good to go but maybe not good enough to wave wheel. Steve went first with a beautiful line. Next Bill, deciding that this waterfall was no match for his skill, went vertical at the top in his Disco and threw the biggest wave wheel ever caught on film at that time. When wave wheeling from this high, it is very important not to land flat. Unfortunately Bill landed flat. It did not bode well when he came out of the bottom of the falls slumped over in his boat. After roping him out carefully and taking him to the same nearby hospital as Todd, the crew learned that Bill had broken his back. I realized how lucky I was to be with the Twitch team.

On the eighth morning everybody woke up early feeling perky. I don't know if it was because we got to sleep inside the previous night or because we knew what an adventure we were about to embark upon. The creek was in an excellent location with the put-in less than ten minutes from Squamish, BC, at the end of Howe Sound. We checked the water level and found it to be slightly lower than the previous day which we hoped would be good.

The first order of business was to remove a log out of the second drop to make it runnable. With prussics, pulleys, and about 40 minutes of grunt labor, it was out of our way. The theme for this creek was "short, but steep." Directly below the put-in was the largest, mellowest drop: a 35-footer into a small pool, which lead directly into the second drop, a small 10-footer with the water seaming into a crack in the middle. These drops went by smoothly, and we made our way to the crux and finale of the run.

The lower section was nothing but gradient. It started out with the burliest 15-footer landing on rocks and backed up by a boulder. A small area of shallow water separated this and a hard left boof into a pothole type pool. Two strokes more and the boater would be heading down a 25-foot, nearly vertical slide into a fair sized pool. Shortly after came the last drop, which necessitated enough speed to ride up on a rock to clear another seam of water falling into a crack.

The whole stretch was all connected and with either a roll, or two wrong strokes, things could get ugly quickly.

It turned out to be a creek with interesting moves and lines. It was so much fun in fact, that we ended up doing repetitive laps on the last three drops with smiles on our faces. When we had had enough of the creek we decided it was time go swimming and rope swinging in the local swimming hole at the bottom. Everybody was laughing and having a great time. After awhile it was time to move on and, of course, get some food in our bellies.

The amount of quality boating we found in such a small radius was impressive. I knew someday I would be back here with friends to do many of the same runs. But on that day, our goal was to find bigger and better whitewater as we searched for our Canadian Twitch fix.

All good things must come to an end. On our ninth day we finally found ourselves leaving the awesome guidance of Stuart and heading east. We met up with Shannon Carroll and Ben Coleman for breakfast in the little town of Mission. After breakfast we headed out towards water, only to find that our new area had none. Bummer. We scouted all day trying desperately to find some water that was paddleable, but were shut down numerous times. Finally we found a creek late in the day that we could paddle the next day--- back in business. I got the inclination that the amount of quality whitewater we paddled every day the previous week was an oddity. We realized even more now, how much Stuart had helped us out, and we were grateful.

On the tenth day we experienced another impressive seven-hour creeking adventure. I learned a valuable lesson---always wear elbow pads when creeking. The run started out fairly low and easy for about five kilometers. We entered the first gorge and the whitewater picked up. The upper section of this run was fun: 10-foot drop after 10-foot drop. There was one drop that looked kind of ugly, but after watching me do it cleanly, everyone else got back in and paddled it.

We finally got to the horizon line of the waterfall that Brandon had scouted the previous day. It was huge and completely walled in.

There was only one micro-eddy at the lip where two people could scout. We knew it was burly when it took Brandon and Tao more than 20 minutes to scout a drop. From the micro eddy I was in, the only thing that could be seen was a pool 70 or 80 feet below. It is quite a feeling knowing that the only way out of a river is through a rapid.

After a long deliberation at the top, Tao said he was going to paddle it. Over the lip he went. All we could do was wait and hope for him to reappear at the bottom. He finally did, was okay, and started narrating back to us via charades what had happened. All we could make of it was that he hit a lot of rocks on the way down. None of us wanted to run it. The only option left was to "half way" run it. This involved a seal launch of about 20 feet, then catching air out and into the bottom of the waterfall's veil 30 feet below, not knowing what was in the landing.

This move was the scariest thing I had ever done in my life; it was also the biggest seal launch I'd ever done. Directly below the falls was a narrow but straight forward 15-footer, a couple of 10-footers, a few small rapids, and finally the take-out. I knew it was more important to stay focused on the moves necessary to make it around this challenge rather than dwelling on the fear aspect. I made it. The run itself was awesome, minus the huge waterfall, but nonetheless I was happy to see the take-out.

After packing up and grabbing a quick dinner we were on our way home. Canada had been very kind to us with incredible whitewater, big waterfalls, perfect weather, and beautiful scenery. I almost regretted leaving this gorgeous, clean, friendly environment. Driving home and pondering my Canadian adventures, I began imagining what my next Canadian trip would be like.

# Chapter 19

## The Philippines: In Search of New Water

The time had come for the third foreign segment of *Still Twitch'n* to be filmed. We had already been to Canada three times and some of the crew had been to Thailand. We wondered where else we could go that was new and unexplored. We received a call from Ned Sickles, one of Tao's old friends that was now running River Quest, a rafting/kayaking company deep within the Philippine Mountains. He told us there were awesome, unexplored rivers all around him. We decided this was where we wanted to be.

The group consisted of four paddlers: Stuart Smith, Tao Berman, Mark, Ken from Wenatchee who had lived in the Philippines years before, and myself. Also in our crew were Eric Link, videographer, Jock Bradley photographer, and our host Ned.

We left Vancouver January 4, 2001 about 2:00 p.m. on Cathay Pacific Airlines for the 14 ½ hour flight via Hong Kong. Arriving in Manila around midnight we learned our boats had not made it on the same plane. The airline offered to book us into a hotel for the night, but with all the bombings that had been going on in the city recently and the fact that our ride was here waiting for us, we decided to head out. They told us that the boats would be shipped directly to us "by and by." This was their way of saying, "Yeah, it will eventually, or probably, happen." We wrote down everyone's names and phone numbers and hoped for the best as we headed out of the airport.

It was awesome to be here. Once we were through the doors, we were immediately enveloped in the warm, sticky odor of a third world country. We walked past the armed guards to our new friend and escort for the trip, Maverick. Maverick looked a little on the shabby side at first; older and worn with not too much tread left in her, and a bit rusty. Maverick was our Jeepni--- a jeep that has been converted into a people hauler with a truck bed welded onto the back of it. We would spend many long days and nights in Maverick. Critter, a raft guide from River Quest, the company we would be staying with, informed us that this Jeepni was one of the nicest in the area. All the others had no tread, patches on the outside of the tires and a lot more rust. We crowded in and began the 250-mile, 14-hour ride to the northern Philippine province of Kalinga.

Critter was only along for the ride and was being dropped off on the outskirts of Manila. He enlightened us with many stories of animal killings, machete slayings, and tribal wars in the area we were traveling to. On our way out of the big city I noticed that red lights, street signs, and lane markers didn't really mean a damn thing; the Filipinos just went through lights once traffic cleared. A four-lane highway meant nothing. Sometimes it was two lanes, sometimes six, with people swerving all over. If a pedestrian was in the way he had better be out of the way before a vehicle got to him. It was awesome! Where in the States can you get away with driving like this? I wished I was at the wheel. On the way out of town we got pulled over by the police; I really didn't know why. The officers didn't even get out of their vehicle. Our drivers walked around the Jeepni a couple times. Critter got out and pissed in the street, and then we were back on our way.

By 3:00 a.m. I had been up nearly 24 hours; I was tired. Of course I hadn't slept too well in the all-metal, windowless, diesel Jeepni that was swerving its way down the road in and out of traffic. Every time I woke up and looked outside there were people everywhere---just hangin' out. I wondered what the hell they were doing. It never got quiet on the streets all night long, even when we were far from the city.

Fourteen hours later we finally arrived at our destination, one of the nicer houses in the middle of the malaria-ridden rice flats. It was a solid concrete building, including the floor, with every window and door wide open, and the refuse pile right out the window. Luckily we would be staying down the road at a huge government hostel with running water, electricity, and most importantly, screens on the windows.

In the time that we were waiting for our boats and gear to arrive we strolled around town and listened to stories from Ned about the Kalinga people. He reiterated how they are really nice people as long as you aren't mining, logging, or damming their resources. We learned that we were in a blackout tourist area; this is an area that outsiders are strongly advised to avoid. Until only 50 years ago these people were known as a band of head hunters. Apparently not too long ago a business came in and tried to dam one of the rivers; rumor has it that the Kalingas massacred them with machetes, leaving their heads on stakes to let others know of the dangers of damming their rivers. Trying to rectify the situation, but mostly help out the company, the government sent in the Army; the Kalinga slaughtered them, too. The government generally stays out of this area now and lets the people be.

While driving around town, every once in awhile I would see an old man with full sleeve tribal tattoos walking around. It was amazing to be around people full of pride for their culture. With my bleached blonde hair, I noticed that I stuck out like a sore thumb. It was almost as if they had never seen anything like it. I got baffled stares, pointed at with screams of "Americano" and huge smiling faces. The rig must have also looked different than the people were used to seeing because we got more stares and yells than my blonde hair did. The people were really nice to us, even though the rest of the country fears this area.

Being anxious for our gear to arrive and start paddling, it was good to wake up the next morning and see our boats stacked on the front porch. The Philippine shipping service worked. They found us in the middle of nowhere all the way from Manila. We packed the

Jeepni full. To help expend pent up energy, I climbed to the thatched roof of the little house the Jeepni was parked next to, jumped to the roof of the vehicle and then to the ground. We finally headed out on our paddling mission.

Carving our way through the high mountains and through many villages we slowly made our way to the water. We were headed for a play run that was only 20 miles away but took two hours to get to. The rivers looked fairly low. Rain could help us out a bit; but it didn't matter because I knew that right then back in the States it was cold and snowy.

When the river wasn't in sight our eyes would wander to the eighth wonder of the world, beautifully shaped rice terraces carved into the mountainsides. The Kalinga had cared for and protected rice terraces and the rest of their land for generations.

It wasn't long after we started unloading gear and getting ready at the put-in that the entire town circled around us. First the children came running to us and slowly all the parents and grandparents were circled around us watching in amazement as we changed and geared up. There was no room for decency here. If they didn't want to see a naked white person then they shouldn't have completely circled around us. All the children giggled and the elders smiled when we made the quick change into our boating shorts. It was probably the first time that most of them had seen a white---well, you know.

After walking on trails that took us around and through some beautiful rice terraces, we were down to the river and in our boats. It had been nine days of traveling, packing, unpacking, and waiting for our boats since we left the States, but we were finally on the river. The day flew by quickly with a few good holes, some great splats, and a lot of fast and furious paddling. We were tired that night. After boating it was back in Maverick for a 19 mile, 2½ hour drive to the top of the mountain where we stayed with one of Ned's friends.

During the night we heard on television, which is a rarity in these high mountain villages, that the Filipinos were trying to impeach the president in Manila. Our hosts thought that a revolution could break out if he wasn't impeached. There could be some interesting times when we got back to Manila.

Waking up the next morning to the sound of wings flapping madly and bodies thumping against each other, I cruised outside only to find our host and drivers training their roosters to fight. They were getting them ready for the weekly Sunday cockfighting event. The main contender every week was the local governor who had over 300 fighting cocks in his front yard. It wasn't considered cruel because the chickens were going to be eaten anyway; they thought it actually gave the chickens more of a chance to have a longer life.

*** 

We made our way to the headwaters of the Sultan river and had one last obstacle to overcome before boating: the local tribal leader. He was the mayor of 13,000 people in a 5500 square kilometer area. All visitors had to stop and talk with him to gain permission to be in his region. Kayaking had never been encountered there before. The locals were a little wary of us, which was not something you wanted in these parts.

We stopped at the mayor's house and described to him exactly what we were doing. We showed him a photo of Tao running a waterfall and he commented, "That looks very dangerous." His smile implied that he thought we were crazy. Looking at the photo, he said he didn't quite understand why we wanted to paddle on his dangerous river but didn't want to hold us back either. He told us he would alert the people in his area about what we were doing so that we wouldn't be hassled while there.

Not only did the mayor wish us luck, but he sent us on our way with a local guide to pass along to others his good will towards us. We scooted on down to the put-in. Again it was in a little village and all the townspeople put everything on hold to come stare at us in bewilderment.

This trip would mark Ken's virgin first descent run. The river was about 13 miles long, with a fair amount of easy Class III that we had seen from the road. For a first descent of this length we probably should have gotten started a little earlier, but because of the slow driving and the talk with the mayor, 12:30 was the best we could do.

The river had plenty of water in it for boating but was low in comparison to its usual flow. We paddled quickly through the flatwater and made good time. Most of the rapids had been created by huge landslides that had fallen into the river leaving behind massive boulders. Low water forced us to trek through the bottom of these boulders. A lot of the rapids had a 90-degree turn in them with slots barely big enough for a boat to get through. Many of the rapids had a bunch of different channels that ended in either a sieve or nasty undercut. Luckily there was always at least one channel that took us past it. It seemed like every rapid had many different places to go but only one route was the correct one; I named one of them Maze Run.

At one point the river ran into a wall and simply stopped. I had never seen anything like it. At this point we were in a gorge which meant portaging was not likely. If the water had been higher there would have been no way around this spot. Luckily since the river was so low there was a triangular cave against the left wall big enough for us to squeeze into and float through. The rest of the water went under the wall. We found many slots and ledges falling off boulders with tight entrances and exits, containing all the obstacles I mentioned. At one rapid Tao got out and told everybody what line to follow. He watched and laughed as every last one of us got worked in the hole in the middle of this double drop; though Tao got spanked too.

It seemed as if we were on some sort of a holy mission, perhaps "The Search for the Sacred Take-out." "There will be many different paths my son, with one and only one being the correct one. Only a true kayaker knows which one path is correct." I kept saying this in my head all day in a sort of medieval wizard's voice as we wove our way down river. Apparently part of this river puzzle was the amount of water, and we had guessed it correctly. My wizard would have crowned us true kayakers.

We must have spent a little too much time chatting with the mayor because the sun was starting to set. About an hour before dark we came to a rapid with a makeshift bamboo bridge across the river, and we knew we wouldn't make it to the take-out before dark. None of us had much food or water left. Assuming there would be a trail from this bridge to the road we decided to leave our boats, hike out, then come back the next day to finish the run.

We started hiking quickly in hopes of being out by dark, but what we thought would be a one hour hike to the road turned into a seven hour hike through the bush in the middle of the night. Our group accidentally split into two groups, each going their own way. I ended up with the group with the flashlight. Trails ended and began everywhere; we lost our trail many times throughout the night. Our goal was to simply keep hiking up towards the road, with or without a trail. Our light went out, but slowly the moon rose high above us. It was the perfect night for such an excursion with the full moon lighting the way, and the temperature in the mid 70's.

I didn't worry about wildlife in this jungle because we knew the Filipinos ate everything. If there was wildlife anywhere near us it would be long gone by the time we got close to it for they were hiding out in fear of being eaten. However some of the group were worried about running into cobras, as they were the first to bushwhack their way through the jungle. We encountered many cliff bands, and we tried to walk around, climb up, or climb a tree to reach the top--- without much success. I climbed one tree trying to get to the top of a cliff only to find out when I got down that I was covered with insects. They bit for what seemed like a couple of hours while I scratched wildly. The itching eventually stopped, or perhaps I just got used to it.

I was starting to think that the other group had already made it to the road and was laughing at us hysterically, when I heard them yelling at us. We yelled back. Once reunited, we told each other stories of how our nights had been thus far. We learned that the other group, led by Tao, had been about 1,000 feet higher than we were, and hadn't found the road. We sat down and started thinking about the possibility of going to sleep and finishing the run in the morning. Half of the group wanted to sleep while the other half wanted to trek on. We argued about what to do and which direction to take.

Bruised, battered, exhausted, and dehydrated, I glanced over the group every once in awhile to see if anyone had reached their breaking point yet--- this is the point when the mind stops thinking logically and starts focusing on survival. Things such as hoarding food and water and yelling can start to occur. I must say that for the most part, we managed to maintain our cool.

After much debate it was finally decided that we would trek on. By some weird coincidence the trail that Ned had said looked better than the numerous trails we had traversed, took us all the way out. We trekked up and up until we spotted a village. Continuing to follow the trail through lush rice terraces, we finally arrived.

It was the middle of the night, and we were a bunch of dirty white guys coming into a small tribal village high in the Philippine mountains. If there was anything scary about the entire ordeal this was it. All the dogs barked wildly and men started to come out of the huts. Ned whispered to me, "Ask if we can have some water." Not knowing why, but not asking questions, I made the request. After a brief silence we were told to come over to the huts where they offered us some water. Later Ned told me it's a tradition there that if a person asks for water and is allowed to drink, the two are bound to protect one another and are now friends for life.

We explained how we had been lost in the bush and just needed to get to the road, all the while guzzling as much water as we were allowed. They told us how to get to the road, which was very close now, so we headed out for the last leg of the trip. This leg was straight uphill and would drain everybody's strength. At the road we found our ride waiting for us. We picked the leeches off our bodies, climbed in the car, and passed out.

We stayed at the vice-mayor's house again the next night and had the best Philippine meal yet. There were about 30 people at the gathering. Not asking what we were eating, I just focused on how good it was. After dark, we were surprised to be treated with a festive program by the local children. The children out-numbered the adults that night. While the adults were dressed in Western-type wear, the boys, ages 8-15, were dressed in a type of loin cloth, orangish in color with stripes and some had sequins on them. The material was draped over their undershorts, and tied in the back so that the material fell to the ground, but did not get in the way of dancing. As the night wore on, the dancing and humidity caused the backs of the older boys to glisten with sweat. The girls, about ages 10-18, were dressed in black blouses, and colorful long wrap around skirts. Most of the skirts had horizontal stripes of orange, green, and lavender shades with small gold bangles. Their hair was banded in a ponytail at the nape of the neck with a colorful orange cloth.

The air was a-buzz with excited chatter in the local dialect. There were clanging tin cymbals that looked like a round larger sized cake pan. Each song had a slightly different rhythm and sound to the cymbals; there were no other instruments. The boys and girls got all of us dancing. We tried to emulate the steps and moves to much laughter. Most of the dances had all of us hopping up and down as we spun around in a large circle, then separated into smaller circles. In between dances an older white-haired tribal man organized the boys and told them what to do for the next dance. The boys sat down in a line using the cymbals like a drum, banging out different rhythms. A lot of fun was had by all. We felt honored that they had invited us to the feast and put on quite the show for us.

In the morning we learned that the entire town had heard about our ordeal and was worried as well. We were quite unsure how to get back to our boats so we found a local guide. On the walk back I noticed a lot of people laughing at us as we went through villages. I would be laughing too if I was in their shoes. Our seven-hour hike the night before was only a 45-minute hike by trail if we hadn't gotten lost. Along the way I recognized several spots where we had been the night before. We finally got back to our boats and geared up to finished the river. Every first descent has its story and this one was no exception.

We knew that the island had tons of great rivers; the problem was most are out in the middle of the bush with no road access. The water dropped drastically in the area and we decided that there probably wouldn't be any water at our next few destinations so we packed up and headed back to Ned's house.

The next morning before heading out we went into town and participated in an hour-long radio interview with the only station in Kalinga. The staff at the station was very excited to have us there and to learn more about kayaking. The Kalingas don't understand the concept of recreation or doing things for personal pleasure. Our hope was to help them understand this concept a little more. We talked about everything from the basics of kayaking to interesting information about their people. After the interview there was excited chattering from the sound booth and the host thanked us profusely.

Immediately after the interview we were off to the nearest airport for a $40 flight to Manila to catch a flight home. We headed home on January 30, a bit earlier than originally planned due to the low water we had encountered. During our four hour layover in Hong Kong we grabbed a taxi and spent a couple of hours walking the crowded, colorful streets of this vibrant city. After a brief but wonderful trip in a tropical paradise, it was back to the dry States and cold Idaho temperatures. Back at home, I anxiously waited for the water to rise again; just waiting and "twitch'n."

Eric released the final product later that year. *Twitch 3: Still Twitch'n* turned out great. Along with fantastic kayaking footage from the US, BC, and southeast Asia was some insane footage of Brandon and Stuart setting a new record dropping the most vertical elevation in under one minute. We ran a flood control canal down a cement chute that was half a mile long. 760 vertical feet were dropped with the landing in only five inches of water. The average pitch of the canal was more than 30 degrees, with some parts even steeper. We borrowed a radar gun from the local police station, and I used it to clock the speeds. Brandon came in at 30.6 mph and Stuart came in at 31.8 mph. Brandon's fastest run was 56 seconds. [8]

# Chapter 20

## More Canadians

In addition to the fine Canadians I paddled with on the Twitch crew, there were other Canadian boaters that I shared adventures with. In 2002 I met Braden Fandrich, owner of Kumsheen Rafting in Lytton, BC, while on a trip to California. He is an excellent kayaker and great guy to be around. Braden was in California with Scott Feindel for the Trinity Rodeo. Scott was hitting up the freestyle circuit and doing lots of training at each of these events. Braden and I wanted to do some river running and playboating, so we headed down the road for a couple of months.

It was mostly just the two of us paddling together except when we met up with the famed New Zealand kayaker, Nikki Kelly, and some other kayakers that we joined for awhile. Braden and I spent some time in Placerville, California with Nikki and her friends and had fun running all sorts of fantastic whitewater. I was quite impressed with her. Later that summer Nikki came to Idaho to kayak and stayed at the townhouse with mom and me.

Braden and I traveled on a shoestring budget. We ran out of gas at least twice. I have video to prove our austere life style: us eating bologna slathered with mustard and ketchup, but no bread. Yummy! My Ford Escort station wagon only had room for one person to sleep in it, so Braden camped out on the pavement in his sleeping bag. After the tough night he was none too happy waking up with my video camera in his face, saying, "Rise and shine, Braden."

Braden and I paddled from the Trinity back up to the Oregon Cup, kayaking the Merced River that flows out of Yosemite, and all the forks of the American, South Fork, South Silver Fork, etc. We had excellent kayaking, without much incident. One time however, there was a small tree sticking out into the water on a slide we were doing. Braden barreled into the tree; and I couldn't avoid slamming into him. All was well in the end.

Braden was with me on the trip to Hard Creek near Riggins, Idaho, along with Lochie Mackenzie from BC and Joe Carberry. We also paddled the North Fork of the Payette at very high water. I think the Canadians were impressed with Idaho rivers. Besides lots of great creeking around BC, other trips we took in Canada that stand out were the Thompson River (the Frog), and Fire Creek. My most memorable trip with Braden and Corey Boux was the North Stein River in BC, which is described later in the book.

One rainy day in Canada when there was nothing better to do, we helped another friend, André Benoit, start up a beater car that had been left behind the winter before by some roommates of my Canadian friends. The car was on its last legs. Jumping on the hood of the car, jumping the cables, trying anything we could think of to get it started, we persisted. Finally we pushed the car down the street with André in his mullet hair-cut at the wheel; it finally chugged to a sluggish start, coughing and sputtering in protest. We followed the car, filming. About a mile down the road the car hit a big speed bump and the hood popped up. The car kept going. I don't know how André could see. Other cars kept a wide berth, the drivers staring at us as if we were crazy. We laughed so hard. These antics along with the trip to Cali with Braden are documented in my film *Broke Hungry and Happy*.

Scott Feindel hailed from Winnipeg and later Calgary. He usually came to the States in April to begin a six-week boating season. Besides California, he kayaked in Washington and Idaho then back up to western Canada. Scott first learned canoeing in summer camps as a child. Later he realized the options were more open to him with kayaking, so he switched over. For him the transition from whitewater canoeing to kayaking wasn't that difficult. The strokes weren't as hard as they were in canoeing and the skills transferred easily. He kayaked 100 days his first year and 200 the second year when he was about 22.

Scott and I did some great creeking near Sacramento. He and I along with other boaters were included in the film *Valhalla, 2001*. Scott, Corey, Braden, André, and I had an exciting trip down Mitchell Creek near Lillooet, BC. There were three drops: a 12 footer, one 15 feet, and the other 30 feet. Above the falls we did a bit of rappelling to portage around a very shallow creek section.

Scott and I ran the Little White Salmon near Hood River, Oregon; that was the first time he had boated this creek. We also boated a two-stage water fall on the Hurley River north of Pemberton, Canada.

# Chapter 21

## Making a Kayak Video

Long kayaking trips can cost a lot of money. Producing and releasing a video can cost even more. There were lots of different types of kayaking videos on the market in 2000, ranging from mellow, instructional, straight kayaking to hardcore new school funfests. Every one of those films took an entire season or more of hard work to become reality. There is much more to it than simply buying a camera and pulling it out at the big drops and play spots. A lot goes into these videos just to end up with a short 30 minutes.

Two basic styles of shooting divided all the videos of that time. The first was how videos like Eric Link's *Twitch* series and instructional videos were shot. The videographer attempts to find a possible shoot by looking at topo maps for hours and trampling through the brush scouting, all the time wary of bears. He is always looking for sweet "eye candy" and will often scout for days before boating, even though there is plenty of water, simply because he feels nothing is good enough for filming at certain locations. Most runs should have been checked out and reviewed before kayaking. Once something with potential is found, the filmer sets up the shots and angles before even gearing up.

The other style of shooting is how videos like *Freshwater* and my videos, *The Revolution I and II*, came together--- simply kayaking every day and documenting it. Sometimes you get good footage, other times not so good. Many filmers mix both styles into their repertoire.

Sometimes extra gear must be brought along such as tripods, boom cams, boom mics, lenses, filters, additional cameras, and batteries. It's important to keep the camera free of water while transporting; a simple solution is a Pelican box and a towel. An ordinary drop can be turned into something quite impressive on screen by finding the best angle, and often the drop can be used more than once in the video.

At times finding an angle is easy. Other times it is almost impossible. Hanging onto a tiny weed while leaning over a cliff to move branches out of the shot is scary but often necessary. Sometimes it involves standing on a sketchy mossy area on a gorge wall above class VI while moving to catch the shot. The videographer moves as fast as possible in order not to miss the boater and to help the boater keep that stoke.

Boaters and filmers usually have a simple way of communicating that the boater is ready through a series of hand signals. If the two can see one another it makes it quite simple. When they can't see each other the camera is simply turned on until the boater appears. This can take up to ten minutes while the filmer sits and stares, worrying whether the boater has gotten into trouble above the drop.

After the boating is finished and the footage has been acquired it's time for the mind-rotting, stressful part of editing and turning raw footage into a final product. Editing is one of the scariest parts of the entire process; maybe even scarier than those vertical pins caught on film. When the filmer/editor first sits down in front of the computer he wants his video to be better in every way shape and form than the other videos on the market. It must be unique and stand out.

So much can and does go wrong when editing--- equipment failure, computer crashes, power outages, human error. When dealing with such a large file on the computer things are bound to happen. This is where a lot of stress comes into play. Everything has to be absolutely perfect. Timing is essential.

Editors spend many 20-hour days staring at the monitor with the same few seconds of video and song playing over and over. Barely eating, sleeping, and never seeing the sun fries the brain. When editing, a person gets in "the zone" and becomes like a zombie thinking about nothing other than the video. Sometimes editors obsess about countless ways to put together a single scene.

At times footage must be bought from other sources. It can come from friends, enemies, or stock footage locations. Shortage of film, the quality of others' film, or necessity of a certain shot factor in to the equation.

Acquiring music is probably the most time consuming and frustrating part of the whole process. All good videos must have a quality soundtrack. Countless hours are spent listening to music and deciding what songs would be perfect. A producer may spend months to ensure enough quality songs are acquired. Most often music will cost money and several persons can own a small percentage of the song. All music used must be cleared legally by each of these people and their permission received. Dealing with a bunch of traveling, egotistical stoners is rough; not unlike dealing with kayakers at times. Often there isn't contact information on the CD and the producer gets nowhere after months of researching. However, securing music for the video need not always cost money. I spent a lot of time researching fledgling bands and was able to find a few willing to let me use their music in my video just for the opportunity to have more exposure for their group. This turned out to be mutually beneficial.

Equipment for a video doesn't come cheaply. Although every year the price of electronics goes down as their capabilities go up, it still costs a bundle to get rolling. A good mini DV camera costs anywhere from $800 to $4000 depending on the model, its features, and your needs. Editing programs are also expensive, but a fairly good one for kayak videos can be found in the same range as cameras. To make a quality video, an effects program should be bought as well. These cost about as much as the editing program.

Along with the software, hardware is needed to get the raw video onto the hard drive for editing.

A CD player, capture card, wires, and cables, and possibly a rendering station can cost as little as $1000 or up to $8000. If a mini DV camera was used, it must be saved onto the computer at a very high resolution in order for the footage to come out as clear as it looked on camera. A minimum sized hard drive for one 30-minute project is around 10 gig. The more effects there are the larger the drive needs to be, perhaps up to 40 gig of space. If a person shoots 16mm, estimate around $100 per roll, or three minutes of film. With actual film the rolls must be processed like photos, then transferred to a digital file for the computer with a special component.

There are many ways to sport costs, but in my case, credit cards took the most of it. Acquiring sponsors is one way to help with the burden of the budget. This can be a tough thing to do when asking them to throw down anywhere from $500 to $10,000 ($20,000 in industries like skiing or skateboarding). The hope is to end up relatively even on production costs including all boating and traveling expenses, duplication of tapes, advertising, and printing the box covers.

Printing the box covers is a special process. The print shop needs to be a very professional, four or six color lay-up shop. Printers may tell you they can do it when they really can't or don't even know what you're talking about. The best and least expensive print shops are the ones that will dub your videos for you as well as print the boxes. These are the types of companies that deal strictly with video production and sales. A box is sent to the printer as a file. There are several different program files that printers accept; each of the different programs is expensive and complicated. Sometimes to get the best out of the box many different professional programs are used simultaneously, each one costing around $500. Without experience in the process, it's easy to mess up.

Once the video is completed and the money tacked onto the credit cards, it's time to make that money back--- and then some. It would be almost impossible for you to contact all of the shops around the world that might be interested in your video--- this is where a distributor comes in. A distributor has contacts with these shops and they usually accept his product as gold. Distributors buy a large quantity of tapes at a low price then turn around and sell the video to retailers at wholesale. Sometimes a video is sold strictly through the distributor and no shops are dealt with directly. Shops dealt with directly buy tapes at wholesale which yields a larger profit margin but fewer tapes sold at a time. The largest profit margin is made when a video is sold directly to the consumer from the producer via the producer's website, but usually only one at a time is sold this way.

People won't buy a video they haven't heard of. Advertising and reviews are important. Advertising is very expensive; costs correlate with how large the ad is and how long it will run. I was fortunate to have reviews written on both my videos in several of the kayaking magazines at the time my videos came out.

Like any other business, it takes a big investment of not only money, but time and hard work as well in order for the venture to pay off. You may think that all the guys making kayaking videos are sliding through life but actually they very well may be struggling to make it. In the end, it's all worth it to have a product that you can be proud of for years to come.

# Chapter 22

## The Revolution I

*The Revolution* was forked out the pockets of Dru, Dan, and myself. Our deep love for the sport and our "fun at all costs" slogan was the driving force behind the video, not money. Most mainstream kayaking videos in the late 90s, early 2000s all followed the same lines: kayaking, kayaking, and more kayaking with the hottest pros of the day. We wanted to put together a film using a different approach: new and (up to this point) little known but excellent kayakers having fun. We never imagined it would become such a great video in the end.

About a week before the annual trade show in Salt Lake, Dru and Dan talked me into putting together our own video. Thus "D-Cubed Productions (Dan, Dru, David) was born. We had plenty of film from all our creeking and first descent adventures in the previous year. At almost all times whether on or off the river, my camera had been locked in hand with a happy trigger finger on the record button. Whether we were kayaking, crashing parties, or just hanging with friends---whatever happened I was ready to catch it on film. We also had crazy footage of our urban kayaking escapades.

Dru, Dan, and I sat down and edited a little teaser on my (at that time) junky editing system in one night. In the morning the video was written down second by second on paper and taken to a professional in Boise where it was made into reality for $160 an hour. We soon had a five-minute teaser, an idea, and an already stacked bill on my credit card.

Despite serious rejection at the trade show we decided to pursue production anyway. We needed to find professional editing equipment. We arranged with some friends to use their equipment in Washington, but it would cost us an arm and a leg. I got a random call from a local post-production marketing company. The owner had seen a flyer posted at one of the record shops in town about music for the video and given me a call about editing. After a few meetings it was decided that the video would be edited on their $60,000 setup---an incredible happening at the last second. Dru and I would put together the rough draft and they would do the effects and titling to give it a professional look.

We didn't have much money for music, so looked for struggling new bands in the Northwest who would be interested in getting exposure for their band for very little to no pay. I had recently been in Seattle and found in the *Seattle Tower Records* local music section a band called Data Phantastiq. We thought it would be perfect for our video. That settled, over the course of two fast weeks the rough draft of *The Revolution* was finished and handed over to the duplicator.

Creativity on the box was just as important as creativity in the video. We came up with the following for the back cover:

"Nutritional Facts: Serving size: 40 minutes, Servings per container: 1. Amount per serving:

| | |
|---|---|
| 1st descents | 37% |
| Urban kayaking | 12% |
| Nasty crash and burn | 6% |
| Heinous swims | 1% |
| Pro kayakers | 0% |
| Sick amateurs | 100% |
| Mayhem | 65% |
| Boredom | 0% |

Ingredients:

Water: Andrew West (preserves freshness), David Norell (provides tartness), Dan Menten (prevents caking), Tyko Issacson (provides body). Whitewater states: Idaho, Oregon, California, Montana, West Virginia, New York, North Carolina, Nebraska).

Serving suggestions: View 1-3 hours before kayaking, or as needed to rejuvenate stoke. For best results turn bass and volume to maximum."

To help defray the costs, we needed to get the word out about the video. Fortunately several kayak magazines at the time wrote reviews of the video and Skip Armstrong helped me develop a website, **www.therevolution.cc**, which remains the website to this day. We advertised the video, had a small video teaser on the site, and bios about the boaters.

The videos arrived back in Boise one day before I left for the new season's rodeo circuit; not a day too late and everything had fallen together perfectly. A great soundtrack, an amazing and different video, and on schedule. Not bad for a few unknowns from Idaho who now had thousands of dollars of debt.

# Chapter 23

## Costa Rica

The beautiful country of Costa Rica beckoned me. I knew it would be the cure for my winter blues. I began to plan a trip for December 2001. In 2003 Skip would move down there and join the Costa Rica Rios river guide company, but I was on my own planning this trip. I knew some boater friends I could meet there and was really stoked. In high school I'd taken advanced placement Spanish, but I was a bit rusty. Mom hired Javier, a young bilingual social worker who worked with her, to tutor me before I left. I drove to Portland with my video camera and two boats to spend a couple of days first with Tyler.

My trip was off to an interesting start before I even got to the airport. My flight was scheduled to leave on Tuesday, November 27. The day before, my not-so-trusty JVC camcorder decided to break down as it had in the past at important times. I researched and looked at several options in the one day I had before the flight left. I decided to simply buy the cheapest one chip in Portland. It turned out to be $460, I could now film when I arrived in Costa Rica.

I packed my two boats and gear into a large bag. The total weight of the boats turned out to be 118 pounds---18 pounds more than the allowed amount. My problems started there. The ticket agent found that there was currently an embargo in Central America on oversized baggage. Apparently flights are so full that time of year that baggage had to be down to a minimum. Long story short, I was on my way to Costa Rica for a month on a paddling trip with gear, a paddle, and *no boats*. I was still excited to arrive in a new country, speak some Spanish, and, most importantly, boat in December. I headed for Los Angeles on United at 5:15 p.m.. After a three hour lay-over, Flight 1877 was off for the 8-1/2 hour flight from LA to San Jose, Costa Rica. The next morning at 8:30 a.m. Costa Rica time, our captain announced we had to circle for awhile as the visibility was poor. If the fog didn't clear we might have to land in another town. Fortunately, that didn't come to pass and as the fog lifted I videotaped the coastline through my window.

San Jose is the capital and largest city in Costa Rica with a total metropolitan area population of over 1.5 million people. I was surprised that it didn't seem more third world. The air was clean, the streets were decent, and driving wasn't too crazy---especially compared to Manila. As soon as I got to a computer I e-mailed my sponsors and friends at various kayaking magazines to see if anyone could help figure out how to get at least one of my boats down to me. I thought I could sell the boat before I left, or ship it back and the embargo would be over by then. Eventually nothing worked out to get my boats down, so I arranged for Tyler to pick them up at the airport and keep them at his house where I had parked my car for the trip.

I took a few minutes to email some friends and my parents. Mom missed me when I was gone, as evidenced by her many emails. On trips such as this one, West Virginia, Canada, the Philippines, etc. I only had a chance to check email about once a week. I asked Mom to try to keep her emails down to no more than one a day. It wasn't that they were long, but there were several short emails in a day. She explained she 'd forget to tell me something, so follow one email with another one. I made a "Mom" folder, not unlike a "junk mail folder." I taught this little trick to Amy too. In Mom's defense, she was managing my business while I was out of town, paying bills out of my checking account, dealing with sponsors and people who were requesting me to send my videos to them, etc.

On the second day I was stoked to run into my Durango friend, Chad Crabtree, when I arrived in Turrialba, 40 miles east of San Jose. He had been in Costa Rica since October. I stayed at Hotel Interamericano, which catered to a lot of kayakers. I scored a mattress on the floor of the unfinished basement for $1.75 a night; the next cheapest room was $4-5 per night. There were the requisite cockroaches and other assorted insects as the window did not have glass in it. Taking video of my room, I filmed a small frog on the windowsill. I was wondering if it was poisonous when it jumped--- and I jumped a foot myself. Fortunately, it disappeared outdoors. By the third day I was getting into a routine of going to bed around 10:00 p.m. and waking up at 7:00.

I found out that the boat problem had happened to others, and not just because of the embargo issue. It appeared to be random however, as kayakers arrived by December 1st with boats, no problem. It was frustrating. I managed to scope a Prijon Luv for the entire time if I needed it. There was an upcoming rodeo, and I could help out with it in exchange. I put a deposit of $50 on my credit card to secure the deal. There were lots of boaters by then and I couldn't wait to get on the water.

I couldn't have picked a better time to visit than December. The weather was sunny and the water beautiful. With an altitude of 2130 feet above sea level, Costa Rica's temperature ranged between 59 and 77 degrees in December. The humidity was fairly high as the rainy season lasted from May through November. Even though it was the low water time of year, there was plenty of water and play all around. The rivers ran very close to town. I hooked up with some quality boaters from Maine. Luckily one day I got to get into a Prozone on a wave. I had some awesome rides in it. The Prijon Luv was slowly growing on me. Every day I had better and better rides in it. One day I found a hole so big that I could loop the Luv boat.

I'd talked to people who said they had only spent $500 in a month in Costa Rica but by my standards, this was spending fairly lavishly. I wasn't sure I believed it because even though I was watching my money like a hawk, by December 3 my cash already seemed to be going pretty fast. I had budgeted $12 per day for everything including food, lodging, and transportation.

Food was pretty good---lots of rice, beans, meats, good bread, and delicious fruit juices. Amazing fresh fruit included mangoes, papaya, bananas, avocado, pineapple, and coconuts. To save money I tried to subsist on rice and beans, avocados, and fruits. Unfortunately the new water bottle filtration system that Dad had given me for the trip got left in the back of my boat in Portland, along with my safety kit. Luckily for me and my budget the water, at least in Turrialba, was potable.

The first week I felt my Spanish was not that good so I spent a lot of time with Americans. It was taking awhile to get back into the swing of verb tenses and such. I really wished I had time to rent a room from a local family and pick up the language, but I didn't. However my Spanish improved day to day and was fairly decent by the middle of my stay in Costa Rica.

Next I traveled to Serapiqui, 50 miles north west of Turrialba, and stayed two days. It is close to Tortuguero National Park and also the Central Volcanic Mountain Range including some active volcanoes. This area was green and lush with vegetation. Besides being a kayaking destination in Costa Rica, this was the gateway to many tourist attractions: canopied rain forest with all sorts of flora and fauna, including monkeys, coatimundis, anteaters, sloths, reptiles and amphibians galore, many species of birds, and they say crocodiles, although we didn't spot any. [9]

It rained really hard off and on the first day and as a consequence, the rivers were raging. I boated the Rio Sucio (meaning "dirty river"), appropriately named especially after the big rains. In fact my eyes stung after boating it. This river flows off the flanks of Volcan Poas and has iron oxides in the water that turn the water a rust color, even at its calmest flows. It was a big river on an old flooded river plane, with huge, continuous rapids.

One rapid in particular was sweet; three members of our group barely skirted between two holes while three others went for a nice surf. I felt right at home in the big water, and my Prijon Luv boat handled alright at first. We also surfed the Pasqua section, which was very bouncy. It was probably the biggest wave that some of our group had surfed. I was stoked to watch them having so much fun.

On my ninth and tenth day in CR, we ran the Rio Serapiqui. Day nine was pretty challenging due to the river being swollen from the recent heavy rains. There was a play spot towards the end, and the whole experience was fun. There were a bunch of Ticos (locals) there shredding. Day ten, the river was about half as low, a lot more defined, with some fun rapids and one good wave. My boat was such a tub, but at least it felt stable in the big water and for downriver boating.

After the river we trekked up to a nearby 30-footer and dropped it. I boofed hard planning on dropping the nose at the end. When I went to throw it down, the boat didn't even budge. I landed totally flat, slightly wrenching my back. It was a bit sore that night and the next day, so I did stretches to try to get it back into shape. The Prijon was not helping my playboating. I missed all my favorite moves---blunts, backstabs, wave wheels, flat-water, and even cart wheeling. That evening we watched some footage and it brought to home how frustrated I was that I didn't have my boats with me. Nevertheless I was getting a fair amount of good footage from all different aspects of my repertoire.

On December 8th, we had the most spectacular run I'd ever done in my life up to that point. The put-in on Rio Toro for this class V gorge was at a beautiful place just below a hydroelectric dam. Every 50-100 meters, big waterfalls poured into a deep canyon composed of bright red river rock. The water was blue contrasted by the green, lush forest. I ended up using some of the footage of this section of the trip later in my second video *The Revolution II: Broke Hungry and Happy*.

In the middle of the run was Recreo Verde, a hot springs resort with food and a bar---it was simply amazing. Kicking back in the natural hot springs, relaxing, and talking with fellow kayakers Karen Roy, Aaron Napoleon, Justin Japs, and Cameron Rae, this really topped off the day.

Ironically, after such a great run in the midst of all the beautiful scenery, the take-out was disgusting. It was a pork factory and pig farm with an almost unbearable stench. And we were serenaded with a cacophony of pigs screaming their last screams.

On December 9th I took a day off from boating and saw some spectacular ruins of an ancient pre-Columbian village called Guayabo. Awesome. Being the largest archaeological site yet found in Costa Rica, most of the home sites, trails, and bridges are unexplored. The 3,000-year-old petroglyphs have not yet been deciphered. The carvings include crocodiles, insects, and jaguars. Evidently the people of this ancient village engineered a complex aqueduct system. The rainwater still runs through these aqueducts. [10]

While there I stumbled across a creek that looked like it would be awesome to run. This day marked the halfway point of my trip. I had spent $180 thus far and had $170 left. I needed to continue to be frugal and save $20 for the airport customs tax in order to get out of the country. I was understanding the language much better--- my Spanish was improving and flowing more easily.

The next day we did a quick run on the Pasqua again. It had rained hard throughout the previous night, continuing into the next day. That afternoon the local creek flash flooded. It was crazy to see massive amounts of water and debris crashing down to the town. Houses started to wash away from the banks. I was very disappointed that I had left my video camera in the shuttle vehicle. However, the next day I got some good footage of the aftermath of the torrential rains.

We went to the "best run in Costa Rica," the Peralta section of the Reventazon River. The amount of water seemed perfect, but due to the recent flash floods, the group was concerned the water level might jump up while we were in the canyon, so we decided not to run it. Returning Tuesday it was a little lower than the previous day but still a good level; not too challenging, and a lot of fun. The play was incredible. True to its meaning "agitated," the waves were huge, super-fast and bouncy. My back hurt a bit from bouncing around in my big boat. As we went down the river, we found that every significant little creek pouring in had flooded the day before like the river itself, which caused the river to be dirty brown with tons of sediment. The last couple of miles had huge rapids. I racked up some sweet eye candy for my video. Unfortunately time was flying and my trip was nearing its end. I only had a few days left until the rodeo then a few days after that before I had to head home.

December 13th started off with a tasty bowl of blackberries and mango in milk along with an avocado sandwich, my usual breakfast. Chad, Aaron, Justin, Brett, Cameron, Mario, and myself headed out for the Peralta section again. Though a meter high that day, it should have still been a good level, but somehow the play wasn't quite as good. On one rapid, several of us were boating Blue Angel style--- one right after another. The wave was pretty big, so it was easy to disappear from sight. One of the boaters accidentally slammed into me when I started surfing the wave. His paddle broke off on my mouth, cutting my lower lip. Everyone eddied out to a sandy beach on river left. Justin and Aaron helped me over to the bank.

Knowing that carnage goes over well in kayak videos, and wanting to document everything on this adventure, I asked the guys to film the damage with my video camera. Although woozy, I didn't yet realize how bad my injury was. I asked them to show me my camera monitor after they had filmed me. They said, "No, you don't want to do that." They knew it was not a pretty sight. I grabbed the camera anyway. When I saw my lower lip hanging in two pieces with the jawbone exposed, I almost lost it. I didn't go into shock, but I began to shake and felt as if I was going to pass out. My friends wisely kept me in my wet suit to try to help me stay warmer. We were worried about infection as the river was very dirty from the recent flooding. Chad took a gauze cloth from our little first aid kit and used the water from our canteens to clean my lip as best he could. My lip throbbed and I grimaced from the pain. They gave me two pain pills that were in the kit.

Luckily, we had the local bad ass, Mario, with us. He turned out to be the biggest asset we could have had. Mario, Chad, and Aaron came up with a game plan to get me out of there. Fortunately, we

were on the correct side of the river to access roads, though we
worried that bridges and roads might have been washed out by the
recent floods. We were in a drainage and started up the channel
looking for help. Chad, Aaron, and Mario took turns holding me up
so I could walk; they wanted me to walk so I would stay awake. They
kept asking me if I was warm enough. The rest of the group waited
with our boats by the river.

The sugar cane reeds stood dense and tall; it felt like we were in a
corn maze. We couldn't really see ahead, so Mario used the paddle
like a machete and laid the cane down as we walked. We later found
out that he used to work in a coffee field and was accustomed to
trudging through the jungle with snakes and other creatures.
Evidently, this area had one of the highest concentrations of
venomous snakes in the world---about 4,000 per hectare.

I tried to remain calm. We finally came upon a farmer in the wet
fields with waist high waders on. He asked if we had seen any snakes;
he seemed surprised when we said no. He informed us he had seen
20 snakes in the last couple of hours. He wore the waders to protect
himself from the Fer-de-lance, a deadly black snake. Often snakes,
such as rattlesnakes are defensive and will only attack if feeling
threatened. The Fer-de-lance on the other hand is aggressive and will
attack even though unprovoked. It can be from six to eight feet long.
[11] We only wore booties and shorts, so hearing about the
prevalence and lethality of these snakes did not inspire confidence.

We told the man our situation and asked if he could drive us to
the nearest town. He said that he didn't have a truck and that all the
bridges were washed out. We pleaded with him anyway. Not knowing
if he was being 100% straightforward with us Chad said, "Show him
your lip, David." When I showed him my injury, the farmer changed
his tune and said, "I know someone who might have a truck." He
took us about 300 yards away to a gated complex of buildings. The
guarded entryway was made of stone pillars and the driveway was
paved. It seemed strange to find this large complex out in the middle
of nowhere; we weren't sure what it was. After repeating our story
about needing a ride to a town, the guard told us in Spanish that it

would take a couple of days to get to town. Again I showed him my lip. He said he would get his boss.

A man impeccably dressed in a business suit, came to speak to us; he was bilingual with excellent English. He offered to drive me to some locals who had a dirt bike and could get me into town despite the washed out roads. By then it was getting late and Chad, Aaron, and Mario had to get back to the rest of the group to boat the remaining 10 miles before dark. They asked me if I was okay being left alone. I was a bit nervous about being out there, not knowing a thing about who these men were, but realized I needed to get to a hospital soon. I said, "I'll be fine," and thanked them for all their help.

I was relieved to finally be on my way to Turrialba. I was transported a short distance by truck when we came to a washed out bridge. The driver took me to a Tico with the dirt bike. I was a little sketched about riding on the back of a dirt bike with a stranger in the middle of Costa Rica. But no matter how cold, nervous, and shaky I felt, I knew I needed medical attention. The whole ordeal probably took about 2 ½ hours.

I later learned from Chad that they ran through the sugarcane trail as fast as they could, adrenaline pounding. Every time Chad heard the sugarcane snap he jumped, thinking it was the dreaded Fer-de-lance snake. They were happy to get back in their boats and get out of there.

My driver took me to the hospital emergency room and was kind enough to wait with me until I got help, which I appreciated greatly. At the hospital nobody spoke English. I had no money or ID with me--- they took down my name and birth date. After a brief wait I was taken into a very cold room. I shivered because I was still wet. Although my Spanish was okay by this time, it was difficult to communicate. At one point they sent in a lady who spoke a bit of English; she told me I had to understand Spanish and asked about allergies.

I kept saying, "El rio es muy sucio," meaning the river is very dirty, as I was worried about infection. Finally they were ready to sew my lip back together. I laid down and decided the best thing would be to close my eyes during the procedure. The shots were a bit painful but totally numbed my lips. Fortunately, next they put a cloth over my eyes that was laced with a sedative of some sort. I was able to relax by taking in deep breaths of the medicated cloth.

The stitching process took about 30 minutes and it seemed to go by quickly. I was fairly nervous but tried to stay calm because I knew it would be better that way. I kept laughing to myself every so often. I didn't understand a word the surgeon said. I was in a foreign country, in a cold room, in my wet gear. It was wild.

When they finished, I did a little more paperwork then headed out. At this point I was under the impression that emergencies were free in this country. I thought the nurse had said I was done. Once outside I decided that I should ask if I needed to come back in a few days. I found out they weren't finished with me and I had been asked to see the cashier. At the cashier's window I didn't understand them and they didn't understand me. I could tell that they wanted me to pay, but I didn't know how much. After some frustration I just stood up. Another patient immediately took the window, and I walked out. I still didn't know if I was supposed to go back for follow-up.

Chad and the group met up with me later that night at the hostel and found out that I was okay. I thought my lip looked crooked and was worried about the healing. Perhaps I would need to have it redone when I got back to Idaho. Luckily, there happened to be a Canadian surgeon staying at the hotel. He told me that the stitches would dissolve, but it looked like they didn't do a very good job lining my lip back straight. He told me to ice it that night and he would look at it again in the morning.

I took some video of my face and narrated the story of what had happened. By the next morning the swelling had gone down a bit. In the long run, the lip healed, looked alright, and there was only a slight scar. Add that to the scar above my eye that I got in the sledding accident when I was 10 and it gave me a ruggedly adventurous demeanor.

After my injury, I took it easy for awhile. The lip had put a damper on the kayaking aspect of my trip, but I determined not to let it get the best of me. After a day of trying to decide whether to have it re-stitched in San Jose, I decided that it was all part of the game and I would just roll with the punches. I looked forward to spending the rest of my trip being a tourist and see some more of the country besides just river valleys.

I met up with a kid from Canada who was friends with some of my Cannuck friends back home. He was talking "aboot" climbing the highest point in Costa Rica then heading to the beach--- both of these things worked out perfectly for me. I hadn't gotten around to doing an overnight hiking trip that year and I really wanted to get to the beach, boat or no boat.

My 18th day was spent packing and bussing 75 miles from Turrialba to San Isidro de General where we stayed in a dingy little hotel. The next morning we headed out at 4:00 a.m. to catch a two-hour bus ride to the village of San Gerardo de Rivas, which is at the base of the mountain Cerro Chirripo.

In contrast to the rain forest of Costa Rica, the higher elevations of this mountain area consist of glacier carved peaks of granite, alpine valleys, and year round freezing weather. This is one of the most popular summits to climb in the country. [12]

We started the 16K hike at 7:30 a.m. Fourteen of those sixteen kilometers were uphill and steep, making it a very gnarly hike. We spent one of the coldest nights ever in a hostel at the top of Cerro Chirripo, at almost 13,000 feet. Wanting to save money I didn't rent a sleeping bag but decided it would be a wise decision to pay the one dollar for renting a blanket. I thought, "What's one cold night?" We fell asleep about 8:00 p.m. It was very cold, but fortunately it didn't hit the mountain's record low of 15 degrees Fahrenheit.

Waking up from a cold and terrible sleep, I was more than ready to hike the 5Ks to the summit at 3:30 a.m. to catch the sunrise. The stars at that altitude were simply amazing. After an incredible view, including both ocean shores of Costa Rica, and a beautiful sunrise, we headed back to base camp 10K down. It was time to get to the bottom of the mountain to catch a bus to San Jose by 4:00 and a bus to the beach after that. The hike back was almost all downhill---I don't know how I did it on the way up. I was glad to have such an experience, but I was pretty sure I wouldn't do it again.

By the time we arrived, we were ready for a little rest and some food. I thought that not boating would save me some money but the entrance fees to the area, the two hotels, and all the buses turned out to be spendy. I hoped I would have enough money to last me through the trip.

After a few errands in San Jose we were on our way to the beach---about a five-hour drive from San Jose. The beach was beautiful; the day was warm and humid, sunny and mellow. I was glad I didn't have a boat here as the waves were tiny. We had a great day of surfing and swimming in the ocean. The stars at night were amazing. Luckily we found a place to pitch my tent for only 500/c ($1) per night. I thought this might be the ticket to make my money last through the end of the trip.

The bus ride to and from Tamarindo, a small but high priced tourist town, was really expensive compared to other local buses, but well worth it. Tamarindo was situated in the Guanacaste Region in the Northwest of Costa Rica. There were tons of tourists there. I was sitting in the same awesome hotel that Brett paid for the first night here, sunburned and ready to get home. I scored a free room that night with fellow kayakers, which worked out perfectly. I finished off the trip with a very delicious avocado and cheese sandwich while listening to soothing, classical music in the background. And my lip was okay. It looked like they did a good job after all.

I ended up a bit short on money at the end of the trip, but not bad. I had to withdraw an additional c/2000 (about $6) out of my debit account to cover the $20 airport fees, and gas money to drive the 430 miles back to Boise from Portland. My flight left Sunday, December 23 at 10:00 a.m. and arrived in Portland that same evening at 8:15 p.m.

After spending the night at Tyler's house, I would be driving home on Christmas Eve morning--- just in time to celebrate

Christmas with the family. I was excited that Amy and Travis were going to be with us for the holiday. They all admired my mid-winter deep tan, and I showed off the scar on my lip. I had had a fantastic trip and had lots of tales to tell, with some gifts for all from Costa Rica. And I ended up with over six hours of video. All was well…

David, 1 year old

David practices his karate kick

David, his dad, and Jenny

David and Tyler Smith
train hopping

David arrives at
Ft. Lewis College

Jordan Dew, David,
& Suean off to W.
Virigina

Spirit Falls, David

David's logo

Costa Rica
Carnage

Andrew West,
Dan Menten,
Tyko Isaacson

Urban Kayaking

**Right:** Cannibal Gorge,
David

David and sister Amy,
Christmas 2002

David's 21st Birthday

Difficult portage,
Kaweah River trip

Climax, David 2002
Taken by Jim Grossman

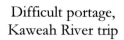

David buys truck from
Grandpa Bromfield

**Above:** Cover of
Kayak Session,
Cheakamus BC,
K. Croy
photographer

**Left:** David and
niece Anna
"I'm scared,
Uncle David!"

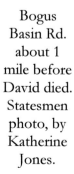

Bogus
Basin Rd.
about 1
mile before
David died.
Statesmen
photo, by
Katherine
Jones.

Friends of David BBQ: Andrea, Lindsey, Dru, Skip, Rae Ann, July 2004

**Right:** David's sister and family: Ben, Travis, Amy, Josef & Anna

**Below:** David's nephew, Josef David, playing baseball, age 6. Looks like his Uncle!

David baseball, age 6

# Chapter 24

## Corey Volt

Dan, Dru, and I were playboating at the Murtagh section of the Snake River near Twin Falls, Idaho in the summer of 2000 when I met a 16 year old red-headed kayaker watching us kayak with a huge grin on his face. He and his uncle were from Ogden, Utah. Soon we were talking and a great day of playboating ensued. Corey had started kayaking at 13. Over the next few years we did some creekin' together on the Payettes, and met up at the Jackson Hole Rodeo. By then Corey was sponsored by Teva, and later by Dagger.

On another trip Corey, Eric Freeburg, and I scouted Malad Gorge and Devil's Punch Bowl. The day was dry and hot, not a cloud in the sky. Unfortunately the water was too low to boat, however we witnessed a spectacular sight. Although there was stagnant water in the pool, the riverbed above Devil's Punch Bowl was bone dry. The Punch Bowl was a large, still pool of turquoise-green water at the bottom of a 60-foot cliff, which was usually fed from the riverbed above. Normally there was a roaring waterfall dropping into the bowl. We noticed a small trickle of water way above the cliff starting to ebb it's way slowly down the creek bed towards the plunge. I filmed as we watched this amazing natural phenomena occurring before our eyes.

That day it had rained hard and it took a long time for the rain waters to begin to trickle down the dry creek bed. We were so excited watching the pool below and the creek bed above, waiting for the first droplet of water to hit the still surface.

"Wow!" I exclaimed. "This is sweet!"

"Dang, dude, it's totally going to fill up!" Corey said. We eagerly anticipated the first little ping at the bottom of Devil's Punch Bowl.

"Oh yeah, dude! Here it comes!" I yelled.

It took some time, but when that first tiny droplet hit the pool below I let out an excited whoop. Amazing. Within minutes the trickle grew in strength to a small stream, and soon a huge waterfall roared down the cliff again. I had never seen anything like it.

In February 2002 I headed down to Salt Lake City to look for work with the Winter Olympics. Corey's family graciously allowed me to crash at their house in Ogden, about a 35 mile drive from SLC. I landed two jobs, one as banquet server at a hotel for Coca-Cola Executives at $8.50 an hour no tips, and the other job was valet parking at $4.00 per hour plus tips. I put in 85 plus hours between the two jobs. Because of all the hours I was working, at times I spent a chilled night sleeping in my car.

Later I got a job taking down the bleachers used for the Olympics. I stashed away quite a chunk of money for the next kayaking season. Even though I was working so many hours I had a blast. I got to see a little bit of the crowds and events. I also got video of some awesome break-dancers.

I witnessed some excitement towards the end of the Olympics. There actually was a beer garden set up near Main Street and the Medals Plaza, which was somewhat surprising to me since Utah is not known as an alcohol-drinking state. When the beer ran out, there was a bit of a melee and the crowd got ugly. A mob scene erupted and police shot some kind of foam tipped bullets to disperse the angry crowd. Twenty people were arrested.

I also had fun with Corey filming stunts of urban kayaking in Ogden. We shot some funny scenes of him kayaking down a snow hill, landing face first into a wire fence. We went down some stairs at the physical education building at Weber State University. People walked by staring at us as if we were nuts. After conquering the stairs, we found some steeper stairs with hand railings. Corey did a great job sliding down the railings in the kayak, landing some of those drops successfully; always with a maniacal laugh when he landed. At one point a police officer came by, and we were worried what would happen. Fortunately, he was merely looking for a truck that had recently driven down those same stairs. These scenes were used in my *Revolution II* video.

Corey tried to get his record-setting 21-stair handrail stunt in the *Guinness Book of World Records*, but they didn't accept it. He said that it probably was because riding kayaks down rails was too new, and we were the first ones to do it.

# Chapter 25

## Revolution II: Broke Hungry and Happy

2002 was a damn good year. I got in some incredible paddling, was financially stable with no bills owed, and did tons of traveling. I placed second in the local Idaho rodeo landing a prize of $300. Jay Moffatt and I, along with the other Pryanha team members, got to hop in the company vehicle for a month of free gas and a ride to some awesome kayaking missions. We boated in northern Idaho, Montana, central Washington, Jackson Hole, and back in central Cali.

The Salmon River Canyon, dubbed the Mount Everest of Oregon kayaking, by cinematographer Brent Buntyn, requires a level of commitment that few are willing to accept. According to *Oregon Kayaking*, Tim Gross and others ran the canyon in 2001. Frustration Falls is the gnarly section of this canyon that kept paddlers at bay. The river "drops about sixty feet over three tiers, with the third drop landing in a 'room' with undercut walls. It's particularly contentious at high flows when the water divides below the first tier, and if the flows become too high, the secondary falls coming in just downstream of the main drop blocks the exit from the 'room.'" Downstream from the room a 20-foot falls gives way to the treacherous Final Falls, an 80-foot drop that had never been run prior to our trip on May 11, 2002. Swimming is not an option there.

These are the issues that had kept paddlers out of this canyon at higher water, but all that changed when Ben Stookesberry, Eric

Seymour, and I completed the first no-portage descent of this river canyon at the highest flows up to that time. We all got pounded hard trying to get out of the "room." Ben was the first one, and the only one on this trip to run this monstrous 80-foot drop. [13]

Since *The Revolution I* video was released a year earlier, I had filmed a lot of new eye candy including the Frustration Falls trip and other missions in Washington, Oregon, California, Idaho, Utah, British Columbia (Whistler and surroundings), and Costa Rica. Most of the filming was from 2002. The time had come for me to put together another video. This time I would be doing the work alone since Dru was enrolled full time in a linesman school. I missed him a lot in the endeavor, but this time I had experience after putting together *The Revolution I*. I knew about the long hours staring at the computer screen to get every scene just right. The editing was much easier for my second film due to the $2800 investment I had made into a new Mac computer with a much better video editing software program. I knew about the details necessary to obtain music, knew about jackets, distributors, marketing and such. Also I felt had matured a lot as a video producer.

I came up with the title *Broke Hungry and Happy: The Revolution II*. The jacket summed it up: "Come along on a journey inside the minds and lives of true paddlers. *Broke Hungry and Happy* depicts what really happens on the river with expert paddlers: deep canyons, huge water, big waterfalls, good lines, bad lines, technical portages, nervousness, emotions between comrades, and the willingness to drop into an unknown waterway or rapid before anybody else. It all comes down to one thing in the end---kayaking!! Not just a kayaking movie, a way of life." The primary featured kayakers (in addition to myself) were Dan Menten, Andrew West, Matt Elam, André Benoit, Corey Boux, Braden Fandrich, Scott Feindel, Corey Volt, and Ben Stookesberry.

I had a bit of fun putting in the non-kayaking extras such as bungee jumping off the King Hill Bridge which stands 170 feet high over the Snake River , with Dustin Urizar and friends. In addition there was break dancing, small scooters jumping over friends lying on the road, a house on fire, bar tenders juggling bottles of booze, an extremely cross-eyed barber shaving a friend's neck with a straight razor, and hot wiring a beat up car in Canada. Of course, the video includes plenty of extreme kayaking including Log Jam Alley in Canada, play waves, rappelling ourselves and boats down steep cliffs, seaweed around our necks and on our heads (Dru and David), etc.

I came up with an idea for the opening with a little help from friends Dru, Justin my roommate, and Nicole Fulfer. To the tune of the opening of the movie *Shaft*, I walked down Main Street in Boise, moving to the beat. I sported dark glasses, a long black trench coat, black slacks, and a nice beige sweater Mom had given me the previous Christmas. My hair was black this time around as opposed to bleached blonde as in "Rev I".

Along the way I came across friend Justin, shook his hand and chatted briefly, then came across friend Nicole and gave her a hug. Rounding the corner I spotted Dru who looked sketchy standing there in a baseball cap with his pit-bull. We shook hands; I looked the dog over, examined his teeth, nodded my head, and handed Dru an envelope. Looking inside the envelope, he glanced around furtively and handed me the dog. I walked off with the dog, and as I passed a dumpster took out a paper plate with a supposedly used slice of pizza on it (of course placed there by me beforehand), took the plate, and walked off eating the pizza. Arriving at my Ford Escort with two kayaks on top of it, I put the dog in the car and sped off. The scene nicely depicted the title *Broke Hungry and Happy*.

We also had fun putting together one section in the middle of the movie that had a lot of people thinking Dru died. It stated: "Dedicated to the loss of a soul. Dru West, I miss you." I showed some of his baby and childhood photos along with his senior picture. Then I had close-ups of myself wearing a Carrera baseball cap backwards, looking very mournful, with tears rolling down my cheeks. This scene required several takes with my camera and the help of copious eye drops to achieve the effect I wanted. Of course Dru hadn't died, but I was expressing how much I missed him since he had moved to California to work full time as a linesman. Naturally there was a lot less time available to him for kayaking.

Mom was pleasantly surprised to find her name in the credits at the end of the film. After the credits came the words "Be careful out there," followed by major carnage: a close up shot of my lip split in two with a deep, bloody gash. Not to be viewed while eating! As a sales incentive I included free red and white *Broke Hungry and Happy* bumper stickers with each purchase of the video. Skip updated my website to advertise the film, and I added a new product for purchase---a tee shirt with Revolution on the front, and Broke Hungry and Happy on the back. There were two choices of shirts--- white with red lettering, or black with red lettering.

This film was copyrighted under my new business name, Dangerous Dave, LLC, and released in early spring 2003. In addition to VHS, I had the film available in DVD form. DVDs had been around since 1996, but were just beginning to go mainstream. When Rev came out DVDs were a bit more costly to produce, and more expensive than the average kayaker was willing to pay. Also at that time more people owned VCRs and hadn't bought DVD players yet. This time around I more than broke even and didn't have to go quite as far in debt to accomplish the video.

# Chapter 26

## Time to Pay Rent

The time had come for me to spread my wings. I resisted moving out of Mom's place because I liked to save money, not spend it, and apartments weren't that cheap. After dating a few years, Mom and Howard had decided to move in together. Mom wanted a bigger house so bought a new home in Meridian, a suburb of Boise. I had to be out by July 15th, 2002. She didn't think having her 23-year-old son living with them would be the best way to get their new arrangement off the ground. She said that I needed to find a place to live, or if I wanted to live with her, that I could pay her rent. I said, "I'm not going to pay rent to family." She countered, "That's my point. So you need to move out."

Moving day came, and I had designed a nice card with pictures of me for Mom. Mom and Dad appreciated the various cards I designed for them; I knew she saved every one of them. The card said:

Mom,

I just wanted to let you know how much I have enjoyed living with you and how much I appreciate your kindness and love over the years, allowing me to stay at your house. I just realized how much I must like living here when I started packing. It is now time for me to push myself and move on in life. I want you to know that you were an integral part of this portion of my life and what I might amount to in the future.

I love you,

David

There was a little heart with flowers on the card. Mom melted when I gave it to her.

The first place I moved into was the back yard of an older house that my friends Byl and Jared were renting. They charged me $50 a month to pitch a tent in the yard and share the kitchen and rest of the house during the day. It was a nice place despite tall weeds in the front yard and the porch sporting an old sofa with the stuffing falling out of it. Dad gave me a nice 9x12 tent that I could stand up in. Mom gave me a folding chair and a plastic set of drawers to keep my clothing in.

Byl was almost a foot taller than I and had joint custody of his one-year-old son. He was devoted dad and used to bring Kaidyn over to the townhouse. Mom taught me to sew while we lived in the townhouse, and she gave me her old sewing machine. I decided to make a pair of pants for Kaidyn; not using a pattern they turned out too big. By the time he could fit into them (girth wise) they were too short because he had inherited the "tall gene" from his dad.

I also sewed myself a pair of gray cargo pants with blue stripes; the legs could zip off turning the pants into shorts. Mom said it was an ambitious pattern for a beginner, especially since I designed it, but they came out well.

Byl got frustrated with me at times because he would come home from work and find I had moved all the living room furniture to the side so I could put cardboard on the floor to use for break-dancing. I used to tape a large piece of cardboard to half of Mom's garage floor so that I could break-dance at the townhouse as well. I enjoyed break-dancing because it's crazy fun and requires a lot of energy and coordination. One of my friends, Marcus Pierce, inspired me as he was a talented break-dancer.

I had to find a warmer place to live (and thus more expensive) by the time winter set in. In November I rented a room for $200 a month in a nice older home on Franklin near Fifth Street in downtown Boise. My roommate Justin impressed me because he was in training and aspired to be a professional biker. Justin was also extremely flexible as he didn't charge rent if I was out of town for a long period kayaking. I lived there until fall of 2003.

# Chapter 27

## Graham Wright

Another good friend of mine, Graham Wright, got into kayaking through a boating experience with his father, Tim Wright. Tim bought a cataraft and invited Graham to go down the South Fork of the Payette; Tim had never been on that river. It was 3500 cfs that day, and the cataraft flipped on a rapid named Bronco Billy. Graham and his dad got the boat upright and climbed safely back on it. The fun wasn't over though; they flipped again on Staircase, and Graham tells me his father was suctioned to the bottom of the river and almost drowned. Graham maneuvered the boat by himself through Class IV rapids and got his dad back on the raft when he eventually surfaced. Although frightening, Graham felt the experience was awesome, and he became hooked on the river. Having seen a lot of kayakers surfing waves and catching eddies that day, he knew that was where he needed to be. Graham was 20.

Graham and I started kayaking a lot together in 2002, one and a half years after his epiphany on the Payette with his dad. We met through a mutual friend, Kelli Ramp. Six months after we began kayaking I remembered Graham and I met skateboarding downtown when we were about 13. We still skateboarded, and even though he was the better boarder, he liked to pick my brain about skateboarding.

I often picked up cigarette butts, beer, pop cans and other trash to clean up along the riverbanks. I couldn't understand how people, especially kayakers, could show such little respect for the beauty of these rivers. I was passionate enough about the subject to write an article about it for *American Whitewater Magazine* in fall 2002. Graham wasn't too thrilled about my passion though because I often put the trash in the back of his truck and he ended up having to throw it away.

On May 24, 2002, two days after my 22nd birthday, Graham and I were going to paddle Boulder Creek, south of Riggins, Idaho. It's part of the drainage from The Seven Devils area. We met a man who asked, "You guys aren't going to paddle that are you? It's dangerous." We told him we were. In retrospect maybe we should have listened to him.

I was planning as usual to get some good footage, so started out by filming an intro to the trip. I said, "Here we are at Boulder Creek, which flows into the Little Salmon. How do you feel Graham?" He said, "Nervous. There's a lot of wood." I said , "Looks like the water's pretty high, eh?" (Notice my little Canadian affectation.) "I'm excited." I added, "Could be challenging!" Little did we know.

It turned out to be a very difficult day. We had to portage every couple of minutes due to all the logs in the river.

And there was a consistent gradient of 250 feet per mile. The water rose as we went down, eddies getting smaller and the brush heavier. There was nothing but choked out sieves and portages. We tried to catch a micro-eddy by the bank to get out. We had to negotiate some dangerous rapids that had low hanging logs we could barely slip under.

About three-fourths of a mile into the run we considered bagging the trip, hiking out, and calling it a day. After climbing up the mountain a bit to see about this possibility, we were discouraged to see peak after peak and figured we were at least five miles to a road. We had to go down the river as best we could--- there was no other option. With his boat falling off his shoulder, Graham yelled and threw his helmet on the ground. He told me he was already exhausted. I knew Graham was really struggling, and I didn't want him to freak out. He had to pull it together to get out safely. I tried to instill some confidence in him, and we hiked back down to continue down the river.

Every portage was at least a half-mile, on steep, crumbling, granite terrain. The task was not made easier in our neoprene booties. We only kayaked two and one-half miles of this creek and did nine miles of treacherous hiking. We got lost trying to portage. We thought we were following the river, but the creek actually took us far from it. We weren't able to see where we were going because we were breaking trail through six-foot tall brush. And to make it worse, we had to do it with the accompaniment of thunder and lightning.

Tired and cold from the rain, we finally came upon a road and a rustic two-story log cabin. Before heading home I stopped and took the opportunity to describe our day on film. "Someone told us this creek was good," I said. "And it was *not* good!" Graham chimed in, "It was so bad!" I said, "It's dinner time, 10 hours later and five miles further---two of which we were given a ride by a guy we found out here in a log cabin."

Graham didn't give up on me. We paddled three to four days each week. After Boulder Creek we ran all three drops on the Little Salmon. It was an awesome trip. Everyone was saying, "You can't run that," but we did.

Graham asked me, "How do you know this isn't going to sieve out?" I tossed a large piece of driftwood into the river to help determine the outcome if we boated it. On the third drop, Graham rolled twice. It was one of the biggest drops he'd accomplished thus far. He did a good job. Afterwards we strung out our gear, ate lunch, and basked in our glory as people came by asking what we had just boated---and they were impressed.

I talked Graham into running all the drops of the Middle Fork of the Payette, above Crouch, Idaho. He didn't want to at first. I think he was scared.

He said, "There's this one 'must-make' move; if you miss it, you're finished." I said, "You paddle hard, you're looking good, you're solid Graham. You can do it!" I would never talk someone into something I thought they couldn't handle, or they thought they couldn't handle.

The creek was high, running 350 cfs. A giant log sieve ran across the entire creek; we had to fight to get around it on the left side. After that it was okay. I think Graham was hyperventilating. Later he said, "Dave, I'd never do it again at this flow; it wasn't fun." A few weeks later we came back at 75 cfs, and it was a good run that time.

Graham and I ran into Jim Grossman, on the North Fork (Payette). He is an expert kayaker and photographer, as well. The day after running the North Fork together, Jim wanted to do the Middle Fork of the Salmon in one day. We put in at 8:00 in the morning. There was still snow and Graham didn't have neoprene gloves or booties. He had borrowed some gloves with holes in them. His hands were frozen within five minutes after putting in. He made frequent stops to warm his hands so Jim and I got ahead of him by quite a bit.

We took out 12 hours later at 8:00 p.m. at the confluence of the Main, after boating 120 meandering river miles in one day. Our shuttle hadn't shown up. Luckily, we ran into a man who owned some wilderness rental cabins and explained our situation. He gave us a ride into the little town of Salmon and we found our shuttle drivers there. They hadn't been able to find us in the dark.

Graham also did some urban kayaking with me. In fact he suggested I kayak down a man-made rocky falls that framed the entrance to an upscale neighborhood in the Boise foothills called Quail Ridge. That footage can be seen in my *Revolution II* DVD. Graham and I also had fun boogie boarding together on the Boise River.

# Chapter 28

## Arizona

Mom was born in Tucson and even though she settled in the Northwest at the age of 22, she always considered herself a Southwestern "girl." She invited me to fly to Arizona with her to see Grandpa in February 2003. This was my second trip to Safford, the first was when I was 14. That was a good visit because Grandma was there too and also my aunt Lisa. We toured the huge Phelps Dodge Morenci copper mine, located on the scenic Coronado Trail, about an hour northeast of Safford. The open pit mine is the largest copper mining operation in North America, and one of the largest copper mines in the world. On the way back we visited the little town of Clifton, where the Apache Chief Geronimo was born in 1819.

This year I missed my grandmother a lot. She had passed away of pancreatic cancer in the fall of 2002. Grandpa, a spry 80-year-old, was lonely and happy to have us visit. He picked us up at the Tucson airport and we decided to do a little sight-seeing on the way home. We stopped to tour the interesting Biosphere near Oracle, Arizona. It was built to be a closed ecological system, which included an agricultural area, and living and working space to study the interactions between humans, farming and technology with the rest of nature.

Driving on to Safford, the beautiful desert scenery was resplendent with tall Saguaro and other types of cactus. We passed

lots of dry riverbeds, with signs touting Gila River and other "rivers."
Mom suggested an idea for my next video---a joke about kayaking the
Gila River. She envisioned me in my full kayak gear, paddle, helmet,
skirt and all, sitting in the kayak in the middle of some dry river bed,
pretending to kayak, or even with a rope attached to a horse in front
of me. I wasn't sure, but she thought it might be funny.

Everyday Grandpa took us to the mountains, showing us Native
American ruins. He was a volunteer with the Bureau of Land
Management and spent time in the desert at various Native American
sites near Safford on the lookout for people illegally taking artifacts
with them. We explored a 1,000 year old site of the Mogollon Indians
and saw pottery shards strewn about. We were always accompanied
by his faithful dog, Matilda, an Australian healer.

Grandpa owned a nice mobile home in a senior park; he had lots
of friends and activities going on. I enjoyed passing time in the
swimming pool at Grandpa's place. It was a low key, relaxing visit, if
not a bit too laid back for an adrenaline junkie like me.

# Chapter 29

### Remembering Charlie Beavers

I headed for Colorado June 1st, 2003. I wanted to be there to see Amy, Anna, and Travis for Anna's first birthday. Mom flew down, and we met up at Grandpa's house for a couple of days. When I arrived in Denver my Ford Escort station wagon broke down. Immediately I had a sense of déjà vu. The previous summer the Escort engine blew. Hoping to save money, I found a man who did auto mechanics on the side. I hired him and thus my car sat on blocks out of commission for most of the summer. It was very frustrating. Mom wasn't too happy when she let me borrow her car to go kayaking, only to have it returned to her with a big dent in the top. Her car didn't have a kayak rack, and tying four kayaks to the roof did not work out that well.

I was in Colorado specifically to attend a memorial float for my friend and Pyranha team-mate, Charlie Beavers. The float was in two days, and at least a three hour drive from Grandpa's house in Littleton. I was in a bind. Grandpa and I took my car to a mechanic who told us there was a hole in the gas tank, and it wouldn't be worth my time and money to have it fixed.

I wanted to buy a pick-up anyway, and Grandpa was getting ready to trade in his 4x4 1992 Nissan, white pick-up with cab for a newer truck. His old truck would be perfect for my kayaking trips, and I could use the covered cab for camping. I'd saved some money but didn't want to deplete my savings. I was grateful when Mom kicked in some money so Grandpa and I could strike a deal. Mom took a picture of Grandpa and me shaking hands in front of my new truck.

The truck had 87,000 miles when I bought it and it stood me well. I put lots of miles on it and took care of it by getting all the oil and lube work done on time, as well as addressing other mechanical issues. My friend Corey Boux put a kayak rack on the top of the cab, when I was in BC later that summer. Besides kayaking trips, I took my dad that summer to the desert to show him what kind of four-wheeling my truck was capable of. I had fun going out with a four-wheeling group in the desert near Boise. It was amazing what they could do with their rigs.

Thankfully I was able to make it to Steamboat Springs for the memorial. Charlie died in the fall of 2002 in Asheville, NC at the age of 21 from a fall. He was an expert kayaker. It is sad to lose a friend and fellow kayaker especially at such a young age. About 11 of us teammates met to float down the North Fork of Fish Creek with Charlie's ashes, his last river run on "this side." We got a good photo of the group. Dixie-Marree Prickett, the team manager, was there along with myself, Jay Moffatt, Matt Sheridan , Daniel de La Vergne of *Lunch Video Magazine* (LVM), Nate Helms, Ryan Casey, Tommy Hilleke, Freddy Coriel, Justin Beckwith, John Gould, and Kato. We all miss Charlie greatly, but were happy to be able to celebrate his life this way.

# Chapter 30

### The North Stein Experience

British Columbia is a tough place to explore, but not just because of access, grizzly bears, or deep canyons. No, local folklore has it that years ago the Germans had paddled almost every river you could scout, or even mention, and said it was no good.

The North Stein was no different. People have been talking about the North Stein for years---locals, travelers, pro boaters, you name it---eyeing it as a potential creek access to its famous bigger brother, the Stein River. The North Stein too, had the usual story of some Germans paddling it years ago and saying, "Don't go back." Luckily, our group didn't hear about this story until we had our minds set on the adventure.

The main Stein is a classic two to three day run in southern BC's Coast Range. The normal put-in is Stein Lake, accessed only by floatplane. The flight to Stein Lake is nothing short of incredible---huge mountains laced with shining glaciers, amazing cascades, multiple creeks and lakes of varying colors, and a patchwork landscape. Unfortunately the cost of flying into the lake doesn't quite fit into a kayaker's budget except on rare occasions.

In 2002, Braden Fandrich---smooth Canadian all-arounder from Lytton, BC, Corey Boux, a Canadian glamour huckster from Whistler, and myself, a Yank known for getting a bit dangerous at times but coming out sparkling clean, flew in to run the main Stein.

We gazed down at the North Stein: whitewater, and lots of it. It looked incredibly steep from the air and dropped right to the main Stein only two kilometers below the normal put-in at Stein Lake. It also originated closer to the main highway between Lillooet and Pemberton. Maybe there was a logging road that led near its headwaters that started from the highway. This sparked a curiosity in our brains that would stay with us for the entire trip. If the North Stein could be successfully completed, it would open up an alternate and much cheaper access route to this amazing drainage. Also you could float two rivers for less than the price of one.

The dry season of fall 2003 was now upon us. With no boating to be found in the area, scouting out new runs was the only way to satisfy Braden's kayaking urges. The North Stein was still itching at his mind. Borrowing a four-wheeler, he went out to find a way to access the North Stein by vehicle. To his amazement and excitement, he found an old overgrown logging road off the main highway from Lillooet that eventually lead to the backside of the North Stein drainage. From here it would be a five to seven mile hike up and over a pass into the North Stein itself.

Having scouted only one time from an airplane isn't usually the best plan of action for dropping into an unknown, steep waterway, but we were in for the adventure. Our crew was lean and mean, fast and furious. It was July 24 and the river levels in the area were perfect for an undertaking like this; not raging high but not back-jarring low either.

With our boats packed for four days (80+ pounds), the drive into the unknown began.

Thick brush scraping down on both sides of my 4x4 left only a small portion of the windshield that I could see through. The last person on this road must have been Braden the year before on his quad; before that who knows. The road seemed to end many times but we pushed on hoping to get as close to the base of the mountain pass as possible.

We finally arrived at a point where the road ended for sure. Immediately after getting out of the truck we were swarmed by hungry mosquitoes. They followed us for the entire hike to the put-in, some seven kilometers later. Hauling our loaded boats on makeshift backpacks, we sweated profusely to the delight of the mosquitoes. If you knew how to read Braille you could have read random sentences on our bodies from all the bites.

Even in a fog of mosquitoes, we couldn't help but relish the majesty of the environment. Before, we had only seen this alpine beauty from the seat of the plane, but while on this hike we were immersed in it. An enormous green, glacier-carved valley surrounded us. The spring water we drank flowed directly out of the ice fields above and tasted like the lips of an angel. It was a steep, boulder-strewn hike up to the top of the pass. Whether the hike to the put-in took three or five hours was beyond recollection. Time slipped out of our minds as the mosquitoes ate us and we trudged on toward the river. The hike went from a steep climb to a flat, mossy valley to a steep tree covered descent, which, much to our surprise, ended at the put-in. We were on river time, and now that time had finally come. Thankfully there was enough water to float on. Finally we could gain refuge from the onslaught of mosquitoes in our dry-tops.

Now the real adventure started. What lay ahead of us on this creek? How steep was it at river level? Would we portage more than paddle? *Could* we portage when we had to? How many days would it take? Did we have enough food? We drifted around the first bend, ready for whatever would come our way.

The North Stein flows 12 kilometers before reaching the main Stein. After the hike it was nice not to have to contend with pounding class V but to just lay back, relax and enjoy the surroundings. The rest of the first day we slowly drifted 10k through amazing scenery and a few logjams. I found myself singing facetiously, "We love logjams! We love logjams!" In fact we dubbed one place, Logjam Alley. We remembered from the flight the year before that once the action started it didn't stop until the river ended.

We camped at the first major slide we came to which marked the beginning of the slanted, white-filled river that would take us straight to the Stein itself. With about an hour left of daylight we cooked dinner, talked, and counted our mosquito bites. The next day would be our day of reckoning---the mystery of the North Stein unraveled.

Waking up to quality whitewater, an entire day in fact, is why I thank my mother for giving me life. It is hard to imagine an entire day, dawn till dusk, of amazing whitewater, but this is what we found ourselves immersed in on day two of our journey. Two kilometers dropping 900 feet each, and then the upper portions of the main Stein with its big volume slides. These two kilometers on the North Stein were, as Boux put it, "the best creek I've paddled in BC." A granitic paradise much like California, but with the consistency of Norway.

There were nineteen slides and waterfalls growing in size and difficulty as we paddled down, each with a calm pool at the bottom. Standing on the brink of a drop you could see three drops above that had just been paddled and two horizon lines below to come. Four of these 19 drops we portaged. Two of these could probably be paddled if we were closer to help. In fact, our topo map named one of the sections of our trip "Two Days From Help."

Commenting on the few portages that we did, Fandrich said, "The portaging was the easiest I've ever done on a steep creek, or in BC." After all of this came the legendary upper portions of the main Stein River with its big-volume slides. Three days after we started, we were sitting in the resort hot tub at Kumsheen Rafting in Lytton with big meals in our bellies and beers in hand, talking of our adventure and other rivers that we heard the Germans had explored. Maybe they had paddled everything around here, found the area to be so pristine and majestic that they just wanted to keep it a secret. It was a dramatic find for sure. Maybe these stories would lead to more gems. Or maybe the Germans had never paddled the north Stein at all. Who knows?

First descent or not is beside the point. Let it be just as adventurous on the 10th descent as it is on the first. That's why we kayak, anyway. It isn't about the rapids, how big the slides are, or how much portaging we do. It's about the journey itself; the hardships, the friendships, the paddling, and the outcome, all in one.

The money dilemma on the Stein had been solved. In its place an alternate and incredible route had been found. A route so incredible that paddlers who venture there might not only find granite and water, but something about themselves and the true meaning of paddling. I think the Germans would be proud. [14]

# Chapter 31

## IR Big Gun Show

The 2003 IR Big Gun Show, hosted by *Lunch Video Magazine* was just that: big gun's showing what type of bodily contortions they can put themselves through, completely free of the water. With five categories that year and $1000 up for grabs in each of the categories, there was a lot at stake. Everybody was itching to take the "doughlers."

August 25, 2003 was a very sunny, 101-degree day in Boise. The rivers beckoned with their warm waters and big rapids. My favorite play hole was in. So many choices. "Keep those priorities straight, first things first," I told myself. One call inviting me to go boating, then another and another. "I'll try to meet you up there, I have some business to take care of first," I told the person on the other line. But we both knew we wouldn't see each other.

That day was the entry deadline for the IR Big Gun Show. I had to get my video together, along with an introduction of myself explaining  how I set up my own video camera and executed a kick flip off a 20-foot drop on the Cheakamus River in British Columbia. Then I had to mix it together on a tape and get to the post office before 5:00 p.m. to send it to LVM by overnight express. This move could set me up with a thousand dollars, so not boating that day was worth it. I knew the move had a chance at winning. I'd put off sending it in to allow myself maximum time in case I came up with more potential entries.

Setting my camera on a tripod in our weed-filled back yard, I reclined on a chaise lounge, wearing my black and red Revolution tee shirt, swim trunks, and sunglasses. I shot at least 20 takes of my introduction speech. Finally I liked what I said:

> Hey, I'm David Norell; this is my entry for the IR Big Gun Comp. This shot is a kick flip off a waterfall in BC, called "Balls to the Wall." I'm the paddler as well as the videographer---I set up my camera on a tripod. I thought I was going to go over the top, over the handlebars, but ended up not doing that. Instead I ended up catching huge air, landing tail first; a totally awesome drop. This is taking the free-style realm to the down-river realm, the type of thing I like doing and like seeing. I like showing people what we're doing out there. You can try this whether you're a big name or not. It's events like this that help push our sport to the next level.

Adding a little humor at the end, I said, "I hope you like what you see," before getting up and walking away from the camera in a tiny American flag speedo.

The 2003 IR Big Gun Show was a huge success; when I say huge I am talking big air, big carnage, and big money. I was very pleased to say the least, when I won the down-river category for a cool grand in my pocket. I also received a trophy that had a kayak next to a tall gold pig on a golden pedestal--- the pig riding a skateboard.

All of the entrants, and especially the winners, had pushed themselves hard to capture their moves with good video. The winners had spent a lifetime training and paining for their rewards. Two broken ankles for carnage winner John Kiffmeyer, multiple beatings and torn knuckles for myself, many big water beatings for Jimmy Blakeney's huge, perfect, clean donkey flip, and years of practice for Amy Jimmerson's launching backstab. Jock Bradley shot an awesome still photo of Billy Harris who came in first for *Kayak Session's* still prize.

There was also a junior category to help push the hearts and skills of soon-to-be ass-kicking juniors. The loop that winner Nick Klemenski busted, shows he practiced hard and deserved his prize. Instead of cash he received a Huge Experiences School Scholarship. The skills he will learn at this school will probably amount to plenty of cash in the future. I have to hand it to Blakeney and his winning move---one of the highlights of the competition. His head, even bent down, was still more than a foot out of the water, and he landed completely flat on his hull in a perfect front surf.

The Big Gun Show is a different kind of competition. No sitting around in a tight eddy with twenty other paddlers hitting you in the head with their paddles. It's the only event where multiple venues from any country, any move, and virtually any paddler are taken into consideration. Big Gun Show co-organizer Spencer Cooke stated, "Take away the variables of water levels, weather, permits, venues, schedule, etc., and you have an event with no boundaries of how big you can go, where you go, when you go, and who you are." Not to brag, but Spencer also said that my entry was absolutely "sick." He said, " I feel Dave probably would've won, if we had named an overall winner to the whole show. The down-river style takes so much creativity. Plus it takes a lot of scouting to find a 20-foot waterfall that's safe enough to flip upside down off of--- on purpose." [15]

Shortly after the show, I was already thinking about what I could do for next year's contest in 2004. I needed to look for the perfect waterfall for my follow-up entry, knowing that I might have to deal with a bruised face to get the perfect shot. But hey, this is the price we pay to push our sport.

# Chapter 32

## Wrapping up 2003

2003 was my 10th year paddling and my biggest paddling year to date in all ways. Although I traveled less, I spent more time running the incredible rivers of Idaho. It was a big water year for us; the famed Bladder Wave, Bennett's Wave, and the North Fork of the Payette were up around 4000 cfs. This year would also see my biggest expenditures; I wasn't on any payrolls. Basically I lived off my savings from the off season to concentrate on kayaking through the summer and fall. I was more loose with money than in the past, which drained my bankroll.

When winter came I got bored, as I usually did, and wished I was somewhere else where I could kayak. I often told my mom I was going to move to Oregon, California, or even BC, as I felt all my friends had moved away from Boise except during kayak season when lots of them came back to paddle Idaho. I know it wasn't that dire, but maybe the many gray inversion days we had in the valley contributed to my sometimes negative outlook about winter.

When I got back from BC, I didn't have an apartment or a job. I decided to take off to Portland, Tahoe, and California to look for work. I first went to Portland in mid-November and stayed with Tyler and his friends John and Jill. After contacting several people I knew trying to get a lead on a job, I still couldn't find work, so I headed to California to visit Dru. We came back for Thanksgiving, spending that day with my good friend Kasia and her family. After Thanksgiving Dru and I headed back to Cali to take him home and for me to look for work. It was awesome to be back on the road together.

Nothing panned out in California though. I had little money other than savings, and to me that was money that shouldn't be touched. Adding to my disappointment about not finding work, was the fact that a couple of sponsors I thought were on board for my *Revolution III* video I wanted to produce had backed out.

One night while sitting in my truck, hungry and a bit discouraged, I jotted down some of my thoughts: "I have nowhere to go, nobody to talk to, no idea of what tomorrow or the rest of the winter will bring." I didn't know where my life journey was supposed to take me at that time. I felt frazzled from the eight hour drive I just finished and overwhelmed at the thought of the long drive back to Boise. That day it hit me--- "Okay, now I'm officially homeless." For the first time in my life I had no fall back, and I have to admit, it scared me a bit.

After eating dinner and calling Kasia, I felt more optimistic. I got my mind in order and was able to think of other options. Christmas was coming soon and I could stay with Dad while I looked for work and an apartment. I thought to myself, "When the going gets tough, the tough get going, so onward!" I was ready for battle.

After driving all night I arrived in Boise the following evening. I stopped in to see Mom first, exhausted and not feeling well. I had a low-grade fever of 101. Mom suggested I stay overnight at her house, and I gladly took her up on the offer. The next morning I felt much better and headed to Dad's house.

Mom had plans to fly to Denver to visit Amy, Travis, and Anna for Christmas. She'd offered to fly me down, but I had jury duty on December 26. It was my fault though. I'd received two jury duty "invitations" over the summer but was kayaking in BC and elsewhere so asked for extensions. They told me I had to do this jury duty as it was the last one I could get in 2003.

Since Mom wouldn't be in town for Christmas, we had our celebration on the 22nd. With Mom's favorite Christmas music in the background we shared homemade goodies and exchanged presents. One of the gifts she gave me was a book about the Hubbell telescope with fantastic photos of the universe. I had taken a course in astronomy in high school and was always interested in that subject. I enjoyed our evening together.

I spent Christmas day with Dad and my faithful dog Jenny, who was getting pretty old. We had a nice, low key time. As it turned out I didn't get called in for jury duty on the 26th, so if I had a crystal ball I could have gone to Denver anyway.

# Chapter 33

## Looking Forward to a New Year

Things turned around for me right away with the advent of the new year. On January 17th, 2004, I moved into the basement of some friends' house on 23rd Street. I worked nights at Bogus Basin ski area, which landed me a free pass for boarding. In addition, I applied at various local television stations, and was very pleased to be hired early in January by KTVB, the local NBC affiliate. Best of all, the job was as a part time weekend news editor. It fit into my schedule perfectly. Friday evenings I worked there on my own, editing "Seven Days with Channel 7"--- a summary of the week's top news stories--- and the Sunday night show "Sports Extra." Then on Saturday and Sunday evenings I edited the 5 p.m. and 10 p.m. news.

I liked talking to the weatherman to get an idea about what my kayaking was going to be like that week, and of course I always looked up the USGS water levels on line. The staff was very friendly to me. I knew they liked my work when after only one month they offered me a full-time position. Mom was very pleased about this job and wanted me to take the offer so I'd have health insurance. The insurance would have been nice, but I thanked them saying I really only wanted the part-time position so I could kayak.

In February, Scott Lindgren, professional kayaker and video producer, came to Boise premiering his latest production *Burning Time*. The previous summer Scott asked if I'd like to appear in his

video performing a stunt kayaking over an 80-foot drop while on fire.
I pondered it for awhile, not being too fearful of the drop, but
hesitant about being set on fire for the stunt, and graciously declined.
I offered to help out in any other way and was pleased when Scott
invited me to help set up that part of the video and help with safety.

The brave soul who finally agreed to be the "fireyaker" for the
film was Jason Hale. The stunt was executed at Lower Lewis Falls in
Washington. After Jason dressed in fire retardant clothing, he said he
felt like the Michelin Man. Scott had also hired a professional
pyrotechnics specialist from California for safety. Most of the fire
went out during the entrance of the falls, and Jason couldn't roll
because the clothing was too heavy. He got waterlogged swimming to
the base of the falls. Tossing the throw-bag to Jason, I pulled him
out. I'd like to think I encouraged Jason because he immediately did
the stunt a second time. The following run was a success, as was the
video.

Scott and I hung out the evening of the Boise premier of his film.
We discussed the possibility of working together sometime over the
course of the next year. I was very stoked about that as I admired and
respected his work. He and his friends had made a thrill-of-a-lifetime
expedition down the Tsangpo River in China in 2002. This adventure
was documented in a DVD from the Outside Spirit of Adventure
series, entitled *Into the Tsangpo Gorge*, filmed and written by Scott
Lindgren. It was also documented in a book *Hell or High Water* by
Peter Heller.

I'd just compiled a video teaser about my expedition to the North
Stein River in British Columbia during the summer of 2003 with
Braden and Corey. And I'd written an article that was published in
the Spring 2004 edition of *Rapid Magazine* about this adventure, not
to mention my picture being featured on the cover. That was the
second cover shot I had had, along with the Summer 2003 edition of
*Kayak Session*. It was great media exposure for my business and for
sponsorships.

I asked my mom if she had any ideas about some classical music
that would go well with my videos as I usually used other kinds of

music. One of her suggestions was a piece called *The Moldau* written by Czech composer Smetana. It starts slowly and softly representing a small trickling stream that begins high in the mountains, and picks up in volume and speed representing the river's descent, whitewater, and steep canyons, until it finally reaches the ocean. After listening to the piece I thought it would do nicely for my *North Stein Experience* video that I was putting together for the National Paddler Film Festival. Mom came to my apartment one afternoon and I played the video for her; she really liked it. Although I didn't win the contest, the judges gave me kudos on the use of the classical music. I was one of the finalists whose films (*North Stein* and *Idaho Whitewater Wrap Up*) were shown in Lexington, Kentucky.

That spring I read about a reality show called *The Millionaire* that was accepting applications to appear on their show. The winner would get one million dollars. Although I lived frugally, that could have helped me a lot with my kayaking/filming career. Setting up my tripod to make a video for the application, I responded to their questions. "Why do you deserve the money and what would you do with it?" I answered:

I'm young, ambitious, and the money would not be squandered. It would be used effectively over a number of years. I'd grow my business, buy better equipment and continue doing my dream job. Other than that, it wouldn't change my lifestyle a whole lot. It'd definitely put me in a different tax bracket though. I'd invest a lot of it to live on in the future. Maybe I could retire at 35-40 years old. That would be sweet!

When asked if there was anything I *wouldn't* do for the money I said:

I don't really know what I wouldn't do; I'm pretty much of a risk-taking type of guy. I'd hope to be myself, do whatever it takes, and hopefully not regret it in the future.

I also applied for *Fear Factor* that spring.

Another fantastic thing about 2004 was I met a cute girl that I really liked. I was downtown at Old Chicago one night in early

January when a friend of mine introduced me to Lindsey Hazelwood. The name immediately rang a bell. I said, " Do you know Roger Hazelwood?" Roger had been a kayaking buddy of my dad's in the 70s. She said, "He's my dad!" She had heard about my dad too. Our mother's knew each other, as well. We hit it off right away and talked about kayaking all night. It turned out she was a kayaker and had been a raft guide with Cascade Raft and Kayak company for a few summers---the same employer I'd had briefly right out of high school. She was currently a senior at Boise State University majoring in education.

Two days later I invited Lindsey skiing and she accepted the invitation even though she was busy getting ready to graduate and doing her student teaching. One evening I went to her house and while waiting for her to finish her lesson plans, I got restless and started doing summersaults on her bed as she typed at her desk. She turned around and said, "David, what are you doing?" I said, "Come over here and I'll show you." Pretty soon she had abandoned her homework and we were both laughing and doing somersaults on the bed.

In March my mom gave Lindsey and me tickets to a Boise Philharmonic concert in Nampa. After the concert, Lindsey and I stood up and kept clapping when Mom walked out into the auditorium to meet Lindsey for the first time. I think we embarrassed her as by that time we were the only ones clapping. Mom used to get tickets for Dru and me and we always enjoyed those concerts. I'd ask her questions like, "Why do you need a conductor? I think you could do without one," and, "I don't see why all those people take individual bows after each piece." Of course Mom would set me straight. Afterwards she'd take Andrew and me to Chili's for dessert.

I usually met Lindsey on Wednesdays after she finished coaching volleyball, which was part of her student teaching experience. We mountain biked together a lot since I was thinking about competing in a local triathlon on April 24. Mom invited Lindsey and me to a Philharmonic concert on April 23, and she also invited us to a movie on another day that month, but Lindsey was really busy coaching girls' volleyball and preparing for finals, so we couldn't go.

In past relationships some of the girls I dated often had a hard time accepting the lifestyle of a kayaker, and the fact that I might be gone for six months or more each year. Lindsey was a kayaker, and I think she understood. However, I found myself wanting to be around her more. We even talked about camping at Otter Slide campground that summer, close to Lindsey's rafting job. I thought Mom wouldn't mind if I stayed at her house while I worked weekends at KTVB.

***

April was a busy month, but mostly I was stoked because kayaking weather was here. In fact, winter didn't really deter me as I occasionally went kayaking starting in February. I always had a winter job to earn money for the upcoming season. I often worked at AIRE raft company as well as Bogus Basin, and thus could score a free pass to snowboard. Although I liked boarding, my heart wasn't in it with the passion I felt for kayaking. I told my mom, "I wish I was a trust-fund baby," like a few of the year-round kayakers I knew who didn't have to work and could follow the season around the world.

In addition to hanging out with Lindsey and having a part-time job I really enjoyed, I was training for a triathlon by boating, biking, jogging and lifting weights. I was also busy developing some articles for a kayak magazine. One of the articles I was working on compared the cardio benefits of kayaking, snowboarding and biking. I bought a special heart monitor and tracked these activities and the corresponding heart rates on my calendar. For example for a 24-year-old in good shape, a target rate of 80% would be about 157. My average heart rate at Climax was 123, max of 169; Gold's Hole, 108-155. Biking up hill and down, I averaged 140 and a max of 179. Running, up hills and down, 1-hour session, 137 average, high of 169.

On April 10 Mom took me to lunch at Burger and Brew, which was close to my office at KTVB. After lunch I gave her a tour of the station. I introduced her around and showed her the computer equipment I worked with. It was cool being able to impress her.

The biggest event of April, other than the triathlon on the 24th, was my '04 Whitewater Inauguration event at Ha' Penny's. The previous year I used this venue for a successful premiere of my second video *Broke Hungry and Happy: The Revolution II*. This year I had a lot of great sponsors and help from Lindsey and other good friends. We had lots of raffle items. Dad was there, but Mom couldn't come because she had a rehearsal. I had edited my kayak footage from 2003 into a teaser with a preliminary title of *Idaho Whitewater Wrap Up*. I was in the process of finding sponsors to publish and complete this video, which would be my third one. The event earned quite a bit of money to put toward this endeavor, and I was really pleased with the results.

On April 16, I attended Mom's party for her boyfriend, Howard, who would turn 50 while she was on a two-week tour of China. She surprised him with an early party. She liked to "show me off" to her friends, several that I hadn't seen in some time. I was good at schmoozing with the older crowd.

In March and April Mom took me to three movies, Mel Gibson's *The Passion of Christ*, *Touching the Void* (which is about two extreme mountain climbers who face death and have to make life or death decisions; on the web it says "the closer you are to death, the more you realize you are alive"), and another movie that turned out to be a nerdy comedy. Keep in mind winter can get boring for an adrenaline-addict like me, so I settled for going out with Mom from time to time.

Perhaps Mom was a bit lonely for family as my sister and niece lived in Colorado and I was her only progeny in town. She had gotten used to me living with her for four years after her divorce when I turned 18. She told me she missed me. I liked her company since she had always been very supportive of my goal to pursue a career in kayaking, whether it took the form of boating, writing articles for kayak magazines, or filming to make enough money to boat. She got my passion; she understood.

# Chapter 34

## Friday, April 23, 2004

I had so much to get done this weekend, with my KTVB job, the Pole Pedal Paddle Triathlon, hanging with Lindsey, and finishing an article for *Kayak Magazine*. I prepared to pull a couple of all-nighters, but no worries---I'd done it before.

Writing a list of all I had to do, I quickly emailed Mom about some ideas for my 25th birthday which was coming up in a month. She'd asked what I wanted. I suggested money towards a new camera so I could take better photos for sending into magazines, an AAA membership, and/or REI gift certificate.

A couple of weeks previous, I'd emailed Rico at *Paddler/ Kayak Magazine* about my "Cardio Comparison" article in addition to another piece on the "State of Kayaking Videos" and how they need to change. Vids were becoming repetitive again, and kayaking was losing its cool image to the general public. I found a good piece written about the Sawtooth Film Festival, which included a couple major kayaking flicks. The author went on to rag on kayaking pretty hard, and it shed a lot of light on how the public views the sport these days.

I also thought of a piece: "I Kayak, Therefore I Am." I noticed the new breed of kayakers/playboaters didn't realize we were all a family in this sport and that we need to look out for one another at all times. Rico responded that he was interested in all of the essay ideas. I emailed Rico that I would bust out the articles and get them to him by Monday.

Some exciting news came April 23 from my friend Eric Freeburg in NYC. I had been in touch with him for two years. He was a cameraman for the TV series *Survivor*, and that was something I would love to do. Finally my persistence with monthly emails to Eric had paid off when he notified me that they were looking for an assistant cameraman for *Apprentice 2*. The job would start May 3rd in New York City. I had just emailed him my resume earlier in the week.

Friday, April 23, I dropped into Mom's office at 11:30 a.m., plopped down in a chair, stretched out my legs, and said, "Hi Mom." She had told me these surprise visits were the highlight of her week. Sometimes I dropped by more than once a week. Since she moved two years previously to Meridian, four miles from my house, I didn't visit her as often because the price of gas had recently shot up to $2.00 per gallon. Mom's mailing address was still my business mailing address since I tended to move around a lot. Rather than drive to Meridian to get my mail I picked it up weekly at her office, which was closer.

We chatted and she offered to take me to lunch as she usually did when I dropped by. Mom had a busy weekend too as she had concerts that night and the next, and a rehearsal Saturday morning. Then she would be leaving Sunday for a two-week tour of China which she was very excited about. She asked if we could go to the post office first and Barnes & Noble second to get a Mandarin/English dictionary, so we did. She'd worked on the language with some CDs for six months in preparation for her trip. At the book store she also wanted to look for the latest edition of *Rapid Magazine*, which featured me on the cover. I told her to hold off because Mother's Day was coming soon and she was going to get a gift from me involving that cover shot. I'd planned to make a big poster for her. I asked her when Mother's Day was, and she said "It's the day after I get home from China, but we can celebrate a day or two late."

Mom asked where I wanted to eat and I chose Macaroni Grill, a place we didn't usually go. We talked about many things that day. Mom had given me a copy of her trip itinerary, which included a six-day cruise down the Yangtze River. "I read your itinerary for the China trip, and it sounds awesome." We talked about other travels both of us wanted to accomplish. I wanted to go to South America to kayak--- either Chile or Ecuador. Mom had lots of other places she wanted to visit such as Egypt, Peru, and Costa Rica to name a few. She surprised me by saying she was even thinking about an African safari with Overseas Adventure Travel.

We talked about my sister Amy, Travis, and my niece Anna who was 22 months old. Anna was such a sweetie; last summer when they visited I put her in my kayak on Mom's driveway and took her picture. She looked so scared but didn't say anything. Amy and her family were coming to visit in June, and I was really looking forward to seeing them again. I asked her if Amy was expecting yet because I knew they wanted another child. Mom said not yet, to her knowledge, but that it probably would be soon.

I told her I'd sent my resume into *The Apprentice 2* for an assistant cameraman position and I was hopeful something would come of that. I also explained why Lindsey and I couldn't come to her concert that night because Lindsey had to work and I was busy with so many things that weekend. And I shared how excited I was about Lindsey's graduation in three weeks. Mom said, "Be sure to buy her a nice present."

We also talked about how KTVB had approved my vacation request so I could participate in a big kayak event, The Gorge Games, to be held at Washington's White Salmon River, July 12-18. I was really stoked about this event. When the topic changed to my upcoming birthday, Mom said, "I'm planning to give you $100 towards the new camera that you want." I was happy about that and thanked her. I also told her I'd been hired to videotape a wedding, and I was reading up on how to do that.

We talked a lot about the Pole Pedal Paddle Triathlon that was the next day. I still didn't know if I could participate because I had to be at work by 2:00 p.m. and I hadn't found someone to fill in for me at work. Mom encouraged me and said, "Those races often start early, perhaps you'd have time for it. I wish I could be there, but I have a rehearsal tomorrow morning."

I finally said, "Well, I better get going; I have a lot to do today." When we arrived at her office, I got out of my truck to say good-bye. Although I'm usually not a very huggy type of person, I hugged her and we said our "I love yous" because she would be in China for two weeks and we wouldn't see each other till sometime in May. I got in the truck and, glancing at my rear view mirror, saw Mom waving at me as she watched me drive away.

When I got home I had a voice mail from Duane at *The Apprentice* who said, "Hey David, I was really impressed with your resume and website. Please call me so that we can set up a phone interview for Monday to talk about the cameraman opening we have." Incredible!

Later I found out that the race participants were to meet at the footbridge in Barber Park at 7:00 a.m. for the first segment of the race that next morning. I decided I could do the race, get a ride afterwards, and make it to work in time--- although it would be tight. I called Lindsey, Kasia, and Mom two times that night to talk to them about the race, but no one was home and I didn't leave any messages.

I got my gear ready for the race, a whitewater kayak, and accessories such as the skirt, paddle, and life jacket. I wasn't going to wear my helmet because it was flatwater. I'd borrowed a bike for the race and loaded it into my truck along with my gear. I had some power bars, water and Gatorade, the camelback bladder, a gift that Mom had bought for me last Christmas, as well as my new heart monitor and wristwatch. I tried to get to bed as early as possible so I could be mentally and physically rested for the event.

# Chapter 35

## April 24: Pole Pedal Paddle

Sunny and only 38 degrees in the morning, the weather was perfect for a triathlon. I got to the put-in on the Boise River at the Barber Park entrance bright and early to register. I wore my red and white *Revolution, Broke Hungry and Happy* tee shirt and a red bandana on my forehead. Dad was there with his video camera filming leg one, the boating part of the race. Several of my friends were surprised to see me because I hadn't participated in previous years. There were approximately 20 contestants in all. A reporter from *The Idaho Statesman* interviewed various contestants, including myself. I told her I was a kayaker but had been biking a lot lately and that I wanted to push myself to do my best. With the training I'd put in, I thought I had a good chance to place well.

My friend Brett Gleason came in second on the first leg, which consisted of a five and one-half mile stretch of flatwater on the Boise River. I came in third. I probably could have done a better job if I had a down river kayak, but I had a whitewater kayak. Long stretches of flatwater were not my usual thing. Still, there were two more legs of the race left; time for me to improve my standing.

When I got to Ann Morrison Park at the take-out, Joe Carberry, my friend who had also organized the race, said, "Good job Dave! Thanks for showing up!" I rushed to change into dry clothes--- blue shorts and my black Smith eye wear tee shirt, the same one I wore the previous day when I had lunch with Mom. I put on the heart monitor, my camelback bladder filled with water, and my race number. Dad took my truck back to his house, along with my wet clothes. He was going to an air show in Caldwell and wouldn't be staying for the rest of the race since he couldn't really follow us up Bogus Basin Road and be able to see anything.

It had warmed up nicely but fortunately was not too hot for the challenging bike ride ahead of us. I got on my mountain bike and began the three-mile trek through downtown Boise to the bottom of Bogus Basin Road, which leads to the ski resort. From there it was 12 miles, mostly uphill, with a few respite areas that were level or downhill. Originally, after the bike portion, we were supposed to ski; but the snow was rapidly disappearing so the event was switched to a two-mile run.

After biking seven miles up the hill, I glanced at a photographer who was taking a picture of other contestants and me. I rounded the bend and continued my ascent. I approached the eight mile marker, only four more miles to go. This portion of the race was pretty grueling...

# PART II

# Chapter 36

## Tragedy Strikes

I don't know how long I was on the floor after I received the devastating phone call that David had died that morning, but I pulled myself together because I had to find David and be with him. Later phone records reveal that five minutes after Joe's call, I was on the phone trying to find out where David was and then after that notifying close family.

From this point on, through at least the coming week, I was disassociating--- almost like an out-of-body experience---as if I was watching some stranger who looked like me take charge and handle this mind-boggling crisis. I'm sure I couldn't have coped with it any other way.

I called both hospitals to ask if David was there; he wasn't. I called a friend and they suggested calling the Ada County Coroner. A young man answered at the coroner's office. He said yes, David was at the morgue. I said I was coming right over to see him. He said that wasn't possible because it was the weekend. I replied, "I want the name and number of your supervisor."

I finally reached the coroner and repeated my desperate request to come be with my son. He said I couldn't see him until Monday evening at the funeral home.

"You mean I can't see my son for two more days?"

He said, "It's Saturday and we are short-staffed; we aren't set up for a viewing."

I said, "I don't need a viewing, I need to be with my son. He just died!" I felt devastated that I hadn't been there when he died, that he died alone. I didn't know how to do this. I felt his spirit might have been hovering there waiting for me as he lay on the road, but would his spirit wait for me until Monday?

I tried again with the coroner. "I need to identify him." I knew he didn't have his wallet with him during the race.

He said, "He had a race number."

What if it was the wrong number registered to him, and they had the wrong person? I needed to be with David to help the reality set in as well. I later learned that some of his friends, particularly Joe, had been there after it happened and they knew it was David.

The coroner said, "The only way you can see him today is if we don't do an autopsy on Monday."

I said, "No, I want an autopsy." I had to know why he had died, although I knew it was most likely related to the fainting incident ten years ago in high school.

I began the difficult task of notifying loved ones and friends. I called my daughter Amy, but no one was home. I called her mother-in-law Diane and told her the news. She expressed how sorry she was and said Amy was at a friend's house. Due to the fact that Amy was two months pregnant, Diane didn't want to startle her over the phone. I remembered my lunch with David just the day before when he had asked me if Amy was pregnant. I felt sad he never knew, but Amy had asked me to keep it secret a little longer, so she could tell him when she visited us this summer. Diane called Travis, Amy's husband, at work, so he could tell her in person.

Next Diane called Amy's friend to tell her what had happened, but asked her not to tell Amy. It must have been difficult for her friend to keep a happy face, knowing Amy would soon be devastated. When Travis arrived at Amy's friend's house, Amy knew something was wrong. She assumed perhaps a grandparent had died. When he told her David had died, she couldn't believe it. As many people who are in shock react when they receive news like this, she too exclaimed, "Is this a *joke?*"

The next person I called was Mike. No answer. Then I called my 81-year-old father who was snow birding in Safford, Arizona. "Dad, are you sitting down?" He knew right away it was bad news. I told him, and he was shocked. I asked him to call my sister Lisa and my brothers Mark and Calvin. I told him, "I need you here Dad." I knew it would be difficult for him to get to Idaho since he had been planning to leave Arizona that week and head back to his home in Littleton, Colorado. Fortunately a friend in Arizona drove with him to Denver. Then he flew to Boise with my sister. In between calls, I kept calling Mike. I didn't want him to hear about David on the news.

I called and left a message for Roger Hazelwood, Lindsey's dad, to call me right away. Later Mike called him several times, as well. When Roger saw all those messages he worried something had happened to Lindsey and David. Lindsey had started to wonder why David hadn't called her yet. He was supposed to call her right after the race. They'd made arrangements to meet that night after he got off work.

The information spread like wildfire among the kayak community. Several of David's friends were at the site where David died shortly after it happened. Graham Wright and Kelli Jeffress even went to a print shop and had 100 red and white bumper stickers printed which said: "Do it for Dave!" They passed these out to friends.

Lindsey called her mother, a Life Flight nurse at St. Alphonsus, to see if she had heard of an accident involving David. She hadn't. When a friend of Lindsey's finally called her to tell her, she reacted just as Amy and I had, crying out, "Is this a joke?" Lindsey later told me she went on for several hours thinking it was a cruel joke. She called her mother, and her mother tried to comfort her and tell her it was true. Lindsey also said she wished the hospital had known about it because if her mom had been on a helicopter that life flighted David off the mountain, she thinks he might have lived. So do I.

I called my Philharmonic stand partner Kathy, to tell her David had died and asked her to tell our director that I would not be at the concert---the first concert I had missed in 33 years. I also asked Kathy to tell fellow musician Doug Lawrence that I wouldn't be going to China the next day. He was going on the tour as well. I later heard that the news spread somberly throughout the orchestra, right before they went on stage. My friend Melaney found out after she was already on stage and the downbeat was about to start. There were tears streaming down her face as she played the first piece. She and I had raised our two children during the same time, each having one boy and one girl.

Next I called my friend and colleague, Sue Roark, who was also going to China with me, to tell her I wouldn't be taking the trip. I guess I was blubbering and she thought I'd said my dad had died. Finally she asked, "Who died?"

I said, "My son." She was shocked. I said, "Sue, we've planned this a long time, and I want you to go to China and tell me all about it when you get back. I can go another year." She wasn't sure and said she would think about it. We both had purchased trip insurance. I, of course, had purchased it thinking that my elderly father might get sick and I'd have to cancel. I never imagined that my child would die.

About an hour after David was scheduled to work at KTVB, I got a call from his supervisor, Seth Randal. "Is David coming to work today?" he asked. Normally David would have been editing the 5 p.m. news, which was soon to air. This call surprised me because I had asked someone to notify KTVB.

I cried, "Oh! Didn't you know? David died today." Seth was silent for a long time then stammered his condolences and asked what had happened. Later when I was at Mike's telling him the news, KTVB called Howard and asked him to send them a photo of David via email. They called in staff who normally didn't work on Saturdays to write a brief announcement for the 5:00 broadcast. They had time to put together a bigger tribute with some of David's kayaking footage for the 10:00 news.

\*\*\*

I called Mike again. He was finally home. I said, "I'm coming over." He must have wondered what it was about because I would normally say something like, "Are you going to be home for awhile? May I come over?" At this point I was running on pure adrenaline (like David, but for different reasons) and shock. These two things kept me upright.

My heart continued to race, and I drove on auto-pilot. I called Gina Westcott, my good friend and supervisor, and told her. After expressing her shock and sorrow she said, "Where are you?"

I said, "I'm driving over to tell Mike."

She said, "You shouldn't be driving, I'm coming over to get you."

I said, "That's okay, I'm almost there."

Mike was mowing the lawn as I drove up to his house; the house he and I built and lived in with the kids for seven years. I'd never done this before and didn't know how to deliver such catastrophic news. At least he'd hear it in person rather than on the phone like I had. Who knows which is better.

I was blunt and got to the news immediately. "David died!" I cried.

He said, "What?"

I said, "David died, let's go inside." I didn't want the neighbors to watch us. I later regretted how I told Mike. I wish I could have been more polished and broken the news more gently by saying something like, "Come inside, sit down, I have bad news." But I wasn't in my right mind at this point.

We sat on the couch, and I told Mike the whole story as I knew it thus far, which wasn't much. Pretty soon we were both crying and hugging. The doorbell rang and it was Joe, the one who had notified me on the phone. We had never met or heard about Joe. He was another of David's myriad of kayaking friends and colleagues. Joe had known David for 10 years.

Joe was tearful and apologized that he couldn't reach either of us sooner. He didn't know my last name (I had kept Norell), so he had tried to reach Mike for a long time until he found my phone number on the internet. That was about 3:30. Later, after I talked to EMTs and people who came upon David first, I reconstructed that David probably died about 11:15 a.m. even though the time of death was declared at 11:45. By the time the ambulance got there David was gone.

Joe said David was found lying on the road with his bicycle on top of him, having fallen to his left, as if he had gently tipped over. His left foot had not been in the stirrup so perhaps he'd felt faint and had stopped before tipping over. Indeed there were no bumps, bruises, or scrapes to his head. He hadn't been wearing a helmet so there is a chance he stopped before he passed out or died. Several questions haunt me. I wonder if David knew he was in trouble, that he was about to die. I also wonder if he fainted, like he had that time in high school when his blood pressured bottomed and caused him to stop breathing. Alone on the mountain, there would have been no second chance provided by resuscitation. Or did his heart simply stop beating this time? These questions will remain unresolved until I meet David again.

Joe said that there had been a van going up Bogus Basin Road to help contestants who might be in trouble. They came upon David and a man immediately started CPR. 911 was called but it took at least 20 minutes for the EMTs to arrive. The next day I had a long talk with the man who initially performed CPR and thanked him. He said David's eyes were fixed and staring when he got to him, so he was probably already gone before CPR was started. The EMTs continued CPR for about 10 minutes but it was too late. I'll always wonder, if David had been in the city and EMTs were there right away with a deifbrillator, could he have been saved? It's a moot point, but parents who lose a child easily let their minds run with "what ifs." During all of this somber activity the word spread and young people involved in the race, or cheering racers along the way, gathered on the hill and watched the efforts to save our son.

Of course my biggest "what if" was "what if he hadn't been in the race?" How I wished he hadn't. He might be alive today even with the serious congenital heart condition we later found out he had. If I had picked up David as Mike had asked me to, would I have arrived as the coroner's van was taking him down the hill, or would I have arrived while he lay on the road? If so, I would have known it was my son.

The coroner was going to notify us, but Joe wanted to bring the sad news to us because he was a friend and thought it would be easier. The coroner agreed. I imagine it was one of the toughest things Joe ever had to do. Joe told us he took a kayak paddle, broke off one end, and stuck it in the ground on the hill right next to where David fell on the road. The three of us talked and cried together; then Joe left. Later that week I went to see where my son had taken his last breath.

Mike and I floated along aimlessly not sure what to do. We decided to go to the morgue to try to see David. After looking up the address we drove to the coroner's office. I went to the front door and found it locked; the lights were off. I knocked loudly for some time, but no one answered. I went back to the car and we sat helplessly, staring at the large building where our son lay all alone.

Finally we drove back to Mike's house. As I was leaving I saw David's white Revolution tee shirt that he had worn just a few hours ago during the first leg of the race. It was on the fence where Mike had hung it to dry, along with David's kayak skirt. I asked Mike if I could have the tee shirt, and he said yes.

By the time I got home, Amy had finally heard the news. She called me and we cried over the phone. She said they would fly up the next day. My brother Calvin, his wife Helen, and my niece Suzi, would drive up from Denver on Wednesday. Lisa and Dad would fly from Denver the same day. I made hotel reservations for them.

I called a few of my best friends. My sister-in-law was in Florida on vacation and my friend Cyndy was in Denver with her son who is David's age. When she heard the news she said, "I'm going to hold Andrew (her son) a lot this weekend." Mike called Dru with the news; he was in shock but was stoic and philosophical. Then Dru called me the next day crying and saying, "Please apologize to Mike that I sounded so uncaring, but I was in shock." I told him there was no need to apologize. When people lose a loved one it's hard to get into the reality for some time.

Later that night I recalled that my cell phone had rung at 11:15 that morning, interrupting our open rehearsal. I was mortified that I had forgotten to turn the ringer off. I got a few good-natured "boos" from my fellow musicians. Cell phone interruptions during rehearsals or concerts are a definite no-no. Some remembered that phone call and assumed it had been the call to notify me about David.

But I remembered checking my voice mail after rehearsal. Mike was the one who called me. When I returned his call, he had asked, "Can you pick up David after the race and take him to work?"

I'd replied, "Normally I could, but I just got out of rehearsal, and I have a concert tonight. I have to finish packing for China this afternoon. I'm just swamped." I then asked him, "Do you think David should be in this race?" I had started to worry about an incident in high school when he fainted during a sprint. Mike said, "He's really been training and working out. He'll be fine." Little did I know that David had died about a half hour before this conversation.

I was exhausted and drained and went to bed early that night, clutching the tee shirt David had worn that morning and weeping into it. I woke up every hour, my heart breaking over and over again.

# Chapter 37

## Heartache and Celebrations

Sunday morning I woke with a heavy heart. This was the first morning of the rest of my life without David. I was only 56 years old. I remember when my mom died a year and a half before David and I'd sadly thought I might have to wait 30 years to see her again. Thinking about not being able to see David for 30 years was unbearable to me. Parents are not supposed to outlive their children. It wasn't fair. I would have given my life to let David live, but wasn't offered that opportunity. It would be awhile before the question, "Why me, God? Why David, God?" would change to, "Why *not* me? Why *not* David?" I believe these tragedies are random. God did not cause David's death, did not wish it on David. However I still wonder, "Why didn't God prevent David from dying?" It's not for me to know yet.

Sunday morning I opened *The Idaho Statesman* and on the front page of the local section of the newspaper was a big article about David: "Boise Man Dies in Pole Pedal Race." There was a photo of David looking directly at the camera, on his bicycle with a red bandana covering his forehead, dark glasses, his black tee shirt he'd worn to lunch with me two days before, and his camelback bladder. Later I would identify the spot near the seven-mile marker on Bogus Basin Road where this photo was taken. It was less than one mile after the picture was taken that he died.

Katherine Jones of *The Statesman* interviewed David and quoted
him as saying: "I want to have a good time, push myself to do this,
and hope it will come out all right in the end." The irony of this
statement broke my heart. I was so thankful David and I spent two
hours together on Friday. I remembered with sadness hugging David
less than 48 hours previously in the parking lot at my office, and how
I watched him drive off in his truck waving at him until he was out of
sight. Little did I know this was the last time I would see my beloved
son alive on this earth.

The day before, both my cell and landlines started ringing off the
hook with people calling offering condolences and help. Many people
dropped by and brought lasagna, brownies, and other food until my
freezer was full. We were very appreciative, but it was overwhelming.

Ralph and Audrey Lawrence, Doug's parents from my church,
called me early Sunday morning. They asked if I wanted them to visit
me that morning before they left for China. I thanked them but asked
them instead to come over when they returned from the trip. They
suggested the name of a good funeral home, Accent in Meridian. I
had no idea where to start with all of this so was grateful for the
advice.

Ironically just two months before I had visited a funeral home
that had a reputation of being low cost in order to find out expenses
in the event of my death. It was a very undesirable place, and I was so
glad I didn't go there after David died. Howard and I got in the car
and drove to Accent Funeral Home. It was closed, but they had staff
on call. I peeked in the door, and it looked all right. I called Mike and
asked if he was okay with me contacting them. I set up an
appointment for that afternoon.

If one has to make arrangements for a loved one, this place was a
good place to do it. I'd only had one experience at a funeral home in
Littleton helping Dad make arrangements for Mom. The owners
were stuffy, lugubrious, slow-talking, with low, soft voices and just
seemed phony all around. When the man left the room Dad and I
laughed about it. The staff at Accent were casually dressed, genuinely

empathetic, and had complimentary things to say about David's kayaking adventures and such when they found out more about him.

This week was full of events that were all the toughest things I'd ever have to do. This was one of them. How many of us ask our children in their late teens or early 20s if they want to be buried or cremated? Mike and I couldn't fathom David being trapped in a box underground knowing his adrenaline levels and his joy of being free and out in the wilderness, so we chose cremation. Later I would second-guess our decision and I asked Dru if he thought David would have preferred cremation. He said, "Definitely, yes. David wouldn't want to be buried." He added, "I want to be cremated when I die."

We opted for a viewing the next evening, Monday. The memorial service was scheduled for Thursday at the church David grew up in, with the eulogy given by our friend and the pastor, Montie Ralstin, who had known David since he was born. We chose 5:30 p.m. so people could attend after work.

Before Amy arrived Howard and I went to David's apartment to get an idea of how many of his belongings were there. We brought home his Mac computer and his other computer. David loved the Mac because it had an excellent video-editing program on it. I talked to his roommates and asked if they could wait a couple of weeks for us to get his belongings. They said to take all the time we needed. I also asked if I could come back later that week just to sit in David's room, and I was given the "okay".

That afternoon we picked up Amy and her family at the airport. The troops were arriving to give us support. Amy was of course devastated. Now she was an only child and I felt bad that when Mike and I were gone she wouldn't have any direct family to reminisce with about her childhood. Anna was a very verbal, precocious 22 months. She remembered her Uncle David. We have several pictures and video of them together.

She saw all of us crying that week and asked, "Grandma, why are you crying?" I said, "I miss David." She said, "That's okay Grandma, he'll be back."

Amy and I worked on the obituary together and submitted it.
Throughout that week we poured through family videos and selected
highlights for the memorial service. KTVB kindly offered to edit and
put together the film selections we had chosen: some from
babyhood, early elementary, junior high, high school graduation, and
Amy's wedding. We were also going to show some of David's
extreme kayaking DVDs as we knew there would be many kayakers
at the service.

Throughout the week we had to arrange for catering, what we
wanted on the memorial brochure, things we wanted to display on a
table at the altar as well as in the foyer of the church,. and what music
we wanted. Amy and Travis helped select music they knew young
people of David's generation would appreciate. I commented to Amy
it was almost like planning a wedding, except it was with deep
sadness that we had to make all these arrangements. In addition
Travis organized a couple of David's friends and had McCue Sports
make a memorial tee shirt with David's logo on it. I really appreciated
this initiative.

Monday was busy. I went early to David's apartment on 23rd
Street; the bed was unmade and the room was messy as was to be
expected. On the middle of his floor was my China trip itinerary, left
where he had read it just three days before. I took pictures of the
room, and then I lay on David's bed and wept. Eventually I phoned
my office to ask one of our doctors to call in a prescription to help
me sleep. The doctor said he'd already called in a prescription for an
anti-anxiety medication. I told him, "I'm not going to take it during
the day because I want to feel my emotions." He said that was fine,
take one at night as a sleep aid and it did help a bit for that.

After awhile I got up and lovingly cleaned David's room: dusted,
made the bed, folded clothes and put them away. Then I took
another picture of the room and left.

When I got home Channel 6 TV (ABC) called asking if they
could come over and interview Mike and me. I called Mike and he
was okay with it. I thought it was a newspaper interview, but duh,
they had said Channel 6. My brain was not really functioning.

Channel 6 conducted a tasteful interview in my living room and tied in some of David's excellent kayaking footage, so we were pleased with it. Later that week Channel 2 interviewed Mike downtown outside of McCue's Sports store whose marquee said: "We will miss you, David." Channel 7 covered the Friday Memorial Float down the South Fork of the Payette River that had been organized by David's many friends. In all there were five TV segments about David that week. He was in the media a lot before he died and after as well.

Monday afternoon the pastor came over and we were able to laugh and chuckle over antics and happy memories as we shared David's life with him for the eulogy. I also had to take clothes for David's viewing to the funeral home. I chose a new pair of blue jeans he had and a nice sweater David liked that I had given him for Christmas.

***

On Monday the most important and difficult thing planned for the week was the first and last time I would be able to see my beloved son since he died on Saturday. I asked Lindsey if she wanted to come to the funeral home, and she did. I also asked my good friend Jeanne Melton to come for moral support. Mike, of course, would be there. Amy was reticent to go as she wanted to remember David alive and vibrant, and like me, was probably afraid to see him lifeless. I would have invited a few of his best friends, but three of them were flying in from California and Oregon and some were driving from Canada and wouldn't arrive until Wednesday or Thursday. The viewing was set for 5:30 p.m.. The autopsy had been earlier that day and it would be several weeks before we found out the results.

Jeanne and Mike arrived and we drove over to the funeral home to say our good byes to David's earthly body. Lindsey met us there. I was shaking, and, as it had been all week, my heart was still racing and pounding. I asked Jeanne to go in first and tell me how David looked. She came back and quietly said, "He looks like he's sleeping." I girded myself, took a deep breath, and walked in to see my son for the last time on this earth. David lay on a lace-covered table with a white drape covering his body up to his waist. I was so glad I didn't have to see him in a casket. At the first sight of David, I wept and let out a wail that only a mother could, and cried out, "David!! I love you." He did look like he was just sleeping, but of course too still and not breathing. I told Jeanne I would be okay. She left me alone with my son.

I spent time pouring my heart out to David about my love for him and my deep sorrow and telling him how devastated his friends were. I even made a joke about the awful elevator music that was playing in the room. I sat quietly in a chair by his side for a long time. Eventually I stood up, touched his hair again, and said, "David, I love you so much. I'll see you again sweetheart. God, I give him back to you." I wept as I turned around and walked out of the room. I believe in my heart I will see David again. I have faith and hold my hope in 2 Corinthians 5: 1-4: "For we will not be spirits without bodies, but we will put on our new heavenly bodies." David's body will be as beautiful as it was on this earth except it will be perfect, that is, his heart will be perfect.

Lindsey was waiting in the foyer; we hugged each other and cried. She wore a long black skirt and a pretty blouse, with her hair done and subtle make-up. I told her she looked so pretty. She said, "I wanted to dress up for David; he loved this dress. He would tease me about wearing sweats." I said, "Well, he was usually in dirty jeans and old tee shirts!" and we laughed. I went outside to sit with Mike and wait for Lindsey. Mike went in last. Everyone came to my house after, but Mike wanted to walk the three to four miles there and be alone for awhile. To this day, every time I drive past Accent Funeral Home I feel sad and remember the last time David and I were together.

***

Thursday April 29th finally arrived. The day before had been Howard's 50th birthday but I doubt that I remembered to wish him happy birthday. I think Howard understood as his sister's only son had died at the age of 20, several years prior. His sister and her husband were very helpful to me during this difficult time.

We gathered all the things we had been working on throughout the week, the music CDs, the two DVDs of David's childhood and his kayaking, the picture board we'd made, his helmet, life jacket, and the white Revolution tee shirt he wore the day he died. We left early to set everything up, dropping Anna off at Amy's friend Necia's mother's house. Flower arrangements waited at the church. The programs were nice, with a color photo of David on the front, and on the back a link to his website along with a photo of him kayaking.

I wore a black skirt with flowers of pink, turquoise, and pale green, with matching top. Amy wore a pretty black skirt with a nice sweater. It had been an exhausting and emotional week for everyone; shock and adrenaline were the only things holding me up along with the tremendous support of David's friends. We had expected about 200 people but the church was packed to standing room only. The crowd of over 400 spilled into the back and the foyer.

Our family was ushered into a small room to wait and pray, then we walked to the front of the church, the last to be seated. There were about 15 of us, taking up two rows. I steeled myself and took a deep breath. Numb with denial, I stayed composed until the video of David's childhood. There was a scene of David at nine months old, walking in his pajamas with a big smile. My heart ached at this tender memory, and I broke out in a soft wail.

There were also moments of the video that made people laugh: David playing soccer at age six, rolling his eyes and playing the baritone horn at age seven, and when he was trying to get his Brittany Spaniel Jenny to roll over. Next came David's extreme kayaking DVD, along with lots of cheering from his friends and gasps from the non-kayakers at the scenes of boaters dropping over 40-70 foot waterfalls and emerging from tumultuous waves of whitewater.

Montie got the story about David's life perfect. He had researched kayaking so he could explain what was entailed to those not familiar with the sport. He also talked about David's skateboarding off the rails of the church. He prefaced his comments with, "Correct me if I'm wrong," and sure enough, during sharing time, Dru "corrected" Montie on a few technical points and everyone laughed.

Montie also read a thank-you card David had designed and given to Mike and me on Christmas 2002. David wrote:

> As I witness another incredible sunset while returning home from another amazing trip, I start to ponder as I usually do. I know at times it may seem as though I take for granted my lifestyle, life and loved ones. But I wanted to let you know that I don't. Many times while traveling I take a moment to reflect on my pleasures and to realize that it could be much different, and that it is quite different for many people in this world. I would not be who I am today if not for you two. I have seen many beautiful sights and have had the opportunity to live very freely. I realize that it wouldn't be like this if not for my two parents. Thank you very much for raising me in a loving family, good environment and neighborhoods. I feel very fortunate and lucky to have had you for parents. Love, David.

I cherish that card, which also has a picture of my handsome son with his dark brown hair, and beautiful blue eyes.

Jody Goode, a friend of Mike's, read a poem she had written after David died, describing his last race:

### Home is Where My Heart Is

Oh the thrill of the race
Exhilaration coursing through my soul
A heart after God's own heart.

To seek, to find
Chasing the bow in the sky
A promise kept by Him who put it there.

My heart pounding hard upon the path
Anticipation rising fast within me
Like mercury measuring the heat of each day.

That day I left, I was racing Home
My heart not skipping even one beat
One beat there
The next one here.

My race is done
I know I've won
What a blast
I'm Home at last
I'll see you when you get here!

The sharing time was a blessing to me, as was the entire service. Truly, I didn't want the service to end. What parent doesn't enjoy hearing an entire hour on the accomplishments of their child and finding out how much he was loved and by how many. Over a dozen people stepped up to share; mostly David's friends. A couple of parents of David's friends spoke, along with Mike and I.

I was touched and overwhelmed. Many of his friends cried or held back tears as they talked. His friend Tyler Smith revealed that he was "the hobo referred to" in the eulogy who rode the rails with David and Tyler's dog. He said:

"I don't know what I would do if I hadn't had Dave in my life. He gave me more energy and made me happier and helped me have a good outlook on life. Someday I hope to die with my boots on doing something I love; I think it's great Dave was doing things that meant something to him when he died and I love him."

His good friend Dan Menten read a beautiful poem he had written on the flight to Boise. It means so much to me that I placed it in the front of this book. Dan talked about the first day he met Dave at the Payette River when Dave was 15. He thought, "Who is this dude--- this little guy strutting around as if he owned the place, full of confidence?"

Braden Fandrich from BC talked about their California and BC expeditions together and what those meant to him. He and another

Canadian friend, Lochie Mackenzie, had driven all night to get here from Canada. That meant so much to me.

They all focused on David's message to live life to the fullest, to live and pursue your dreams with a passion because, as he would say, "You only live once, so live it!" One young man related how he was shocked to hear David had died on a bicycle; when he heard the news, he assumed David died kayaking. He said, "Now I'm going to give up biking. That little guy got so good at kayaking he couldn't even die from it."

Joe Carberry who wrote the news releases and obituaries for the kayaking magazines and *The Boise Weekly*, spoke at the service:

> I'm the one who organized the race where Dave made his last attempt to top a challenge. One thing about Dave is how many people he brought together all over the west coast. The news traveled fast throughout the US, it's a pretty big deal in the whitewater community. What struck me about Dave the most was that the top of Dave's game was living freely, living unpossessed, living with a lack of monetary concern. He was a great example of living your life the way you want to live it, and I admire him for that.

Tara Sanders said, "Every smile I got from Dave I count as a blessing and I always will." Lindsey got up and through her tears told us how much David loved each one of our immediate family, and how much he meant to her.

Dru shared:

> I want to say thanks to Rae Ann and Mike for having Dave. That guy's the best friend I ever had, and the times that I spent with Dave were among the best in my life. The attitudes we cultivated towards life were the things that have shaped the way I live and the life that I have today. Right now, I am the happiest I've ever been in my life; things are going great. I wanted to thank all of you guys too, because even with Dave's death this has been just a fantastic experience for me, so you know, just all around he's had a good impact on me.

Furthermore, I wanted to say, you could look at it as though wow, it's rough, you know. Dave had new sponsors, his job was going good, and he met a girl that was good. You could say it's a terrible time to go when everything's going right, but I think just the opposite. I think that it's a great time to go when everything's going well in your life. If you're on track and you're doing what you wanna do, and if you die happy like that and you live your life properly, then I think that's the best time you can die. If I could have one wish, it wouldn't be to bring Dave back, it would just be that everybody in here would die the same way as Dave, with their life on track.

Dru went on to add:

When people heard that David died, probably the first thing they thought was that he died kayaking. But it wasn't surprising to me the way he went, because he was methodical, calculating, smart, and safe about his boating. For all the people here and elsewhere who have ever said, "You guys are crazy, you're going to kill yourselves," I just want to say, "Ha! I told you so!" on Dave's behalf.

As I stood in the front of the church, I thanked everyone for coming and for sharing their stories about Dave's life. Since there had been lots of talk about how David lived with little anxiety about money and material possessions, I revealed to them that I had just discovered David had only three dollars in checking, but a few thousand in savings and an IRA. I also asked, "Please remember Mike and me in one year." I had heard how shortly after memorial services, friends and support often disappear.

After I finished speaking, I saw the director of the Boise Philharmonic in the crowd. In a couple of weeks when I returned to the orchestra, he would share with me how much it meant to him to hear the things David's friends said about what David had meant to them.

After the service, there was a receiving line (just like a wedding, right?) where I met more friends of David's who all said touching things. Many of them were crying. I reconnected with his dear friend Kasia and one young woman who had traveled from Montana and said she had a crush on David in high school. I wish I could remember her name. Seth Randal from KTVB stated how much he enjoyed working with David and gave me a journal sharing that journaling had helped him when he had lost a loved one. I appreciated his kindness.

Afterwards we enjoyed talking to more people at the dinner that was catered by the church. My nephews, who owned a local bakery, provided a cake that had a photo of David kayaking transferred on the frosting. When it was time to leave, we packed up and my sadness intensified; I didn't want the evening to end.

We had two more events to look forward to and in which to be surrounded by his loving friends. The next morning was the Memorial Float down the South Fork of the Payette River; that event had been organized by his friends. Saturday night was a fundraiser his friends had organized at a local nightclub, The Blues Bouquet.

Unfortunately Amy and Travis had to leave the next morning because Travis had to get back to work. They had been a huge help and emotional boost to me, and I was going to miss them a lot.

***

I looked forward to the Memorial Float and being with David's friends and fellow kayakers and rafters. The kayaking crowd was so friendly; I hadn't met a kayaker I didn't like. All the energy and the vibe of being around these young men of David's age shored me up. If I could adopt his best friends, I would! We arrived in the morning at the South Fork of the Payette at the Deer Creek put-in, half way between Banks and Crouch, Idaho. The South Fork is a beautiful stretch of scenery. There were some good Class III and maybe even IV rapids at the high levels of water in April. Not being a water person, I wasn't sure if I would raft it or not. I don't swim very well and was afraid of being in a river. I had tubed down the Boise River a couple of times in August, but even that made me nervous. This is probably why David never told me about going over 70-foot waterfalls.

There were at least 50 boaters, possibly more. David's dad was there kayaking. I saw several of David's friends, including Lindsey Hazelwood, Mike Leeds, Brett Gleason and others whom I had not yet had the fortune to meet. I wore the white Revolution tee shirt that David had worn the day he died. A reporter from KTVB did a news story about the event. She asked if I was going, and I said I wasn't sure. I told her that I wasn't very adventurous, but I'd like to do it in honor of David. I sat down by the river; the rushing water infused me with the strength and determination to please David. Back on the bank again, the interview continued. I told the reporter, "I'm going! David would be proud of me. He'd say, 'Way to go Mom!' I hope he's watching down on us."

Cascade Raft and Kayak Company had generously donated the use of some of their rafts. My brother and sister, Calvin and Lisa, and niece Suzi and a couple of other people I didn't know were on the raft along with our guide. Thankfully, they honored me, David's mother, by not making me paddle. I held flowers to put in the river at the take-out, and as I got in the raft, I saw a small rope on the side of the raft next to where I was seated. I asked, "Is this the only thing to hold on to?" That little tidbit ended up in the news piece. As we launched, I saw my dad and Helen up on the road, and I smiled and waved at them.

It was exhilarating and beautiful; I could see why David loved kayaking. I was anxious about a couple of the infamous whitewater spots coming up, particularly the steep one called Staircase. When we got there, we hit a big boulder sitting out in the middle of the river. The raft tilted precariously and two men fell out. We pulled them onboard. I thought I was going to fall out too, and I had a fleeting thought: "How would *that* look in the news? Mother of athlete who died, drowns at his Memorial Float."

We made it safely to the take-out at the confluence where the three sections of the Payette converge. We had a moment of silence to remember David, and we all tossed our flowers into the river. This was very touching. I could see the sign outside the store at Banks that announced, "We'll miss you Dave!"

That night KTVB aired a very nice piece about the day. The co-host said, "David was also a part of our KTVB family as a news editor here. We will miss his spirit of adventure and his enthusiasm. He was loved around here, and we'll miss him very much."

The next day there was a front-page article with a big photo of me smiling and waving in *The Idaho Statesman*. Some people asked, "How could you smile when you were so sad?" I explained that I was waving to my dad on shore, and that I was happy all those people were there to celebrate David's life.

***

Saturday the rest of my family was heading back to Denver. Before dropping Dad and Lisa off at the airport, I took them up to the eight-mile marker on Bogus Basin Road, to see the memorial paddle that Joe Carberry had placed there. This would also be the first time I saw where David died.

As we rounded the bend after the seven-mile marker I looked for a white paddle standing upright on the hillside. We located the spot and placed flowers there. I held a single red rose and Dad took a picture of me sitting at the paddle with the rose. It was so sad to look straight down from the paddle about 10 feet ahead of me and imagine David lying there on the road.

David's friend, Kelli Jeffress, painted a large round saw blade with a scene of a blue river, the sun and mountains. Her boyfriend, Graham Wright, who worked in the concrete business, placed the paddle in the hole at the center of the saw blade, and set some cement around the base to anchor it. Although Kelli's painting has faded over the years, the makeshift memorial is still there seven years later.

My trek to where David died became a pilgrimage for me during good weather. Each year starting on April 24 I bring flowers and sit and talk to David. I place a carefully sealed 8x12 photo of David at the site. In November I take the photo home and replace it the next spring. I also visit the site on his birthday, May 22, and each month until the snow flies. At Christmas I place a wreath around the paddle.

I put Dave's red *Broke Hungry and Happy* sticker on the face of the paddle with his name and dates in black marker. On the back I've written "we love you" and the names of immediate family and some of his friends. Other friends stop by there as well, to pay respects and sometimes leave a note.

At times I walk away from the road to the east side overlooking a valley and yell, "David, it's your mom, I'm here! Are you there? I love you!" I always listen hoping he'll respond someday.

After taking Dad and Lisa to the airport, we said our tearful good byes. I was alone for the first time in a week. However, I had one more event to bolster me; the special fundraiser organized by David's friends, at the Blues Bouquet.

Mike, his sister Susan, her husband Steve, and I arrived early to help set up. Dru, Lindsey, Dan and other good friends also came to help set up the raffle, which Dru would MC. We displayed the photo boards, scrapbooks, and magazines from the memorial service. We had videos of David's to play. A five-dollar cover charge would be contributed to the fundraiser. Also proceeds from the auction of videos, a kayak, some raft trips, David's memorial tee shirt, and other items went to the fundraiser. The doors opened at 9 p.m. and soon the room was packed with people. David's *Broke Hungry and Happy* video elicited lots of cheering. David's second grade teacher came up to talk to me. I was surprised and touched to think that he would remember David after 18 years.

After Dru finished the raffle, I was talking with David's friend, Dustin Urizar. In the middle of our conversation he looked over to the side in concern and there was Dru sitting on a bench weeping. Dustin hurried over and hugged Dru; pretty soon a bunch of us were involved in a group hug and cry.

This reminded me of a young woman who introduced herself to me at the memorial service. Crying, she said how sad she was to lose such a good friend. I told her, "I know it must be tough; I'm 56, and I haven't lost a friend yet." The upbeat events of the week filled everyone with strength and courage; it was good for these young people to reunite with friends they may not have seen in a long time.

It helped shore up the defense mechanisms we need to get through such a tragic loss. It was a bit of unreality, numbness, and distraction from having too much time to think about the reality. I'm sure David's closest friends were all on auto-pilot, as I was. They were in for a few rough months.

Many of us stayed until 2:00 a.m., when I finally drove home by myself. I was exhausted from the week, and felt totally bereft and alone. I cried myself to sleep clutching David's tee shirt.

# Chapter 38

## The Diagnosis

About a week after David died I got a call from the doctor who performed David's autopsy. They had been unable to diagnose what was wrong with David; nothing appeared wrong with his heart. As I knew the test results would affirm, there were no drugs or alcohol in his system. They could not find an explanation for his death. However, not having the expertise in this area, the Coroner's office mailed the medical records, autopsy results, and his heart to a special forensic cardiologist in Washington DC. I'm not sure why we got this special consideration, but I'm glad we did. I've known parents whose young adult child died while sleeping and the autopsy results listed "natural causes." In other words, cause of death unknown. I waited another four weeks for results.

I finally got a call when the diagnosis came in. David was born with a rare heart condition called "atresia" of his left main coronary artery. Atresia means that the artery was incomplete and didn't go anywhere. There were at that time only 30 cases of coronary artery atresia in the medical literature. Thus, during David's nearly 25 years of strenuous physical activities, the blood pumping through his arteries and heart would try to pass through the left artery and have to re-route through the right artery. Consequently the right artery was enlarged.

Supposedly there was no cure for this condition, other than to curtail physical activity. Would we have wanted to know that he had a heart defect so we could monitor his physical activity? I don't think so; we wouldn't want to live in fear, David lived his life with adventure and joy. Considering the abnormality, one pediatrician said he was amazed David lived past his first year. I've read about infants who are born with a serious detectable heart defect and have heart surgery in infancy. Some of those babies die. I would not have wanted David to have surgery and risk dying as an infant---we would have missed the blessing of his 25 years. However, I couldn't help wondering if he hadn't been in that race, how many more wonderful years might he have enjoyed?

The doctor said David probably died instantly and did not know what happened to him. I contacted David's pediatric cardiologist and shared the autopsy results with him. Neither he nor the other doctors attributed David's death to his diagnosis of "neurocardiosyncope" at age 15. However, I think that diagnosis was a symptom of this more serious problem, which even his echocardiogram at age 18 failed to reveal. Perhaps an angiogram would have picked it up, but there wasn't enough reason to call for such an invasive procedure at age 15. I learned from a website called "Parent Heart Watch," an organization for parents whose children died from or live with a heart condition, that there is one common denominator among children with heart problems: dizziness and/or fainting spells during exercise. David experienced this in high school. Although it was very sad to find out the cause of David's death, I was relieved to have an answer.

After Dan found out how David died, he told me about a kayak expedition to the Kaweah River they had taken a couple of years before. There was a lengthy, strenuous portage climbing up and down hills through thick brush, carrying their kayaks and gear. Dan said everyone, including David, was exhausted afterwards. Knowing what he does now about David's heart, Dan wonders how David was able to carry on in the many situations like this one that a kayaker frequently encounters.

# Chapter 39

## Learning to Survive

I settled in to the final three weeks of bereavement leave. I didn't know much about this, but I envisioned lying around the house taking care of myself. There was no time for that. Those three weeks were filled with legal and financial issues. I went to David's two banks, withdrew the money and set up a new account for David called "Live Free" to take care of any outstanding expenses he might have. Mike was a joint owner on the account. David and I had been joint owners on each other's accounts in case something happened to either of us; I had assumed that would have been me. I went to a paralegal and he talked me through probate procedures since David had no will. That was emotionally difficult; we had to obtain copies of the death certificate, which is an ugly document to possess when it's your child's. Mike and I decided to share ownership of the pickup truck David had bought from my dad just 10 months before. During that time David put on over 20,000 miles, back and forth to California, British Columbia, and all over the Northwest.

Then Amy called and tearfully said that David had left his IRA to her; he had started one at age 20 and it had about $2000 in it. I recall that he met with Zach, a young man from Edward Jones, who set up the account for him. He told Zach that he hoped to retire by age 45---a goal that Zach endorsed. As David filled out the forms he asked me, "What does beneficiary mean?" I replied, "It indicates who would inherit a person's money when they die." David said he would leave his money to a particular friend of his. I explained, "Well usually it goes to family or parents so they can have help paying for the funeral." That was the end of the conversation; he never told me who he selected as his beneficiary. I was so happy he left his IRA to Amy because she really appreciated it and it helped her realize how much David loved her.

Amy said she was feeling isolated and lonely and wished she could still be in Boise around family and around David's friends and where he lived and died. She said she was crying a lot and her friends kept asking her, "Why are you crying?" as if they had forgotten or thought she should be over it in two weeks. She'd say, "My brother just died." I made arrangements for her to fly to Boise with Anna around David's birthday, which was three weeks away.

The friends who organized the Blues Bouquet event presented us with $3000, an amazing tribute to David. Yes, David had enough to pay for his own final arrangements, but I know he would have been bummed out to see a large portion of his money going towards his death. We could have handled it too, and never had suggested otherwise, but his friends wanted to do this in honor of David. Two memorial funds were set up, one by his friends Kelli Jeffress, Graham Wright, Ben Stookesberry, and Kasia Mastas, a Kayaking Scholarship for kids at the YMCA; and one by me at the Idaho Rivers United (IRU), an organization committed to protecting Idaho's rivers. I learned later that after David's successful Ha'Penny film preview event, he proudly went to IRU and gave them a check for $100. I wanted to continue that tradition.

About a week later Mike and I drove to David's apartment with his truck and brought most of his stuff to my house, since I had a three-car garage. That was a difficult task with plenty of tears. I kept the bed and dresser in my guest bedroom. We had given him the dresser and bed as well as the computer table. I washed and lovingly folded his clothes and put them in the dresser and/or closet. I kept a couple of unwashed tee shirts so I could remember his smell for awhile. I teared up when I saw the heart monitor, thinking, "Why hadn't it alerted him to his danger?" Maybe it did, but it couldn't have saved him.

Before David's friends left town we gave one of David's kayaks to Dru. I told Lindsey and a few other friends they could take some of his clothes if they wanted. Many did, especially the girls. We gave Lindsey his skateboard because that was something David was planning to teach her. We gave the boogie board to Graham because they had enjoyed many hours boarding on the Boise river together. We gave David's belt with the spikes---from his days of wearing big baggy pants, and chains---to Dru. I had a hard time giving up that belt---David had had it for years. Dru told me that when he first met David, he'd said to David, "Hey, kewl belt!" I told Dru to wear it and take good care of it; I took a picture of the belt.

David had a lot of business paperwork that took me a long time to sort through as I had to do his 2004 taxes, take care of bills, and find out if there were any of his videos out there from his distributors to send back to me or have them continue to sell. It took a few weeks of legwork to sort out all of that. I guess all of this was good because during the day I hardly had a moment to think. He only owed $300 on a credit card, which I paid. I checked with his roommate to make sure his rent was paid up. No one showed up after the mandatory three to four newspaper postings about his estate. The truck, of course, was free and clear.

As soon as I got David's paperwork to the house I searched and found the email from Eric Freeburg who had told David about the cameraman position at *Apprentice 2.* I called to tell him about David. He was shocked and very supportive. I asked him to pass the information on to Duane, who had left a message for David to call for an interview. I didn't want anyone to think David was irresponsible. Eric assured me he would spread the word. He later emailed me Duane's condolences as well. Duane wrote, "I think we might have found a position for David with us."

Eric also wrote:

> On the Sunday after David passed, I was kayaking on the same lake I had kayaked all week, but one thing was different.

The serenity. Instead of windy and cold like it was the entire week, it was calm and peaceful; not a cloud in sight. Looking back, I think that David had a hand in that as a special gift to me.

***

In mid-May we used some of David's money to purchase tickets for Amy and Anna to fly to Boise to participate in David's 25th birthday and Mother's Day. It was great to have them visit again. Amy surprised me with a ring for Mother's Day with three small emeralds. Emeralds are David's birth stone. She had put a lot of thought into this gift. The larger middle stone was flanked by two smaller stones. Amy explained that the two little stones represented the past ---our memories of David's life with us--- and the present---our current grieving process. The middle stone represented the future, when we would be with David again. I was touched with Amy's thoughtfulness and the beautiful symbolism of the ring. I wear it on my left hand, close to my heart.

On May 22, David's 25th birthday, we went to dinner with Lindsey and Mike to Texas Roadhouse. After dinner Lindsey came over and we had a birthday party for David. I served cupcakes with candles. We reminisced and Amy read a favorite passage she liked from a book I had given her about surviving the death of an adult sibling. I read the journal piece I found in David's belongings that I've titled "The Daily Grind" in Chapter 13 of this book. Written when he was about 20, the essay sums up David's lifestyle and philosophy of life. This birthday celebration was a bittersweet occasion.

About a week after Amy returned to Denver, I found a scribbled to-do list among David's paperwork. He'd written Mother's Day on this list. I recalled he told me he was going to make me a gift based on his Spring 2004 cover shot on *Rapid Magazine*. I searched his papers and his computer for an indication of what he had in mind and couldn't find anything. I decided to design my own gift---a poster from the magazine cover. On the cover was a beautiful photo of David in his yellow kayak and yellow helmet coming down a drop in the North Stein River in BC. The magazine name, also in yellow, contrasted nicely with the beautiful dark green foliage along the bank of the river. Beside his photo was the caption "Creekin' Stein River." I removed some text on the bottom right corner to make room for what I was going to add to my poster. David knew I really liked his statement in the article, "Waking up to quality whitewater is why I thank my mother for giving me life." It made me cry to read those words after he died. I placed that at the bottom of the with "Love, David" underneath the quote. On the right hand corner I put, "Happy Mother's Day, May 2004."

I had this made into two 14x11-inch posters. The one mounted on poster board, I took to my office. The other, printed on quality photo paper and framed with a beautiful mat, hangs in my dining room. I don't know if this is exactly what David had in mind, but I like to think that he guided me with the ideas for that poster.

***

My month of bereavement leave flew by in a flash. My boss and co-workers were very supportive. My boss told me I could start back slowly if I needed to, which is what happened. During the first couple of weeks there were days I had to turn around and leave at 10:00 a.m. because I was in too much pain to be productive. Fortunately my room was right across from a shower room. For a few weeks when I felt the need I went in, locked the door, turned out the light, sat on a chair in the room and cried. After awhile I gathered myself together and went back to my desk. Fortunately my job then was mostly administrative, and I didn't have a client case load.

Actually, getting back to work saved me. It was only there that I could begin to last a few minutes, and gradually a few hours, without thinking about David's death. On the way home in the car, I'd break down in tears. I'd even find myself driving down the freeway in tears.

***

Three weeks after David died I got a call for an interview for a high school social worker position. I had forgotten about the application I'd put in a year ago. It was difficult, but I pulled myself together and felt good about the interview although I didn't get the job. I had also applied for a Clinical Supervisor position through my department before David died. The job entailed a promotion and salary increase, plus work I thought I would really enjoy. That interview came up about six weeks after David died. Despite competing against six other people, I got the job. I knew David would be proud of me. The demands of the new job were challenging, but it helped carry me through my grief journey.

I learned to manage my days at work, but the evenings alone at home were another story. Grieving people commonly suffer from what we call in the mental health business "anhedonia," or the lack of being able to enjoy anything, particularly those activities we used to enjoy. This is common in depression. After David died I noticed an interesting phenomenon; I would discuss things in two categories: "before David died" and "after David died." Before he died I enjoyed many things: reading, *Frasier*, movies, walking, playing violin etc. For the first month or two after he passed, I had difficulty participating in any of those activites, although I tried. I couldn't concentrate on or enjoy novels. I bought a lot of books on grieving the loss of a child, but at first could only read prayers, meditations, poems, anything one page or less. I tried watching my favorite show *Frasier* but could not laugh. I tried taking a walk two weeks after he died, but less than half a block from home, I turned around and went back. I was upset because May was cloudy and dreary. Then the first sunny and beautiful day I was upset because here was a sunny, gorgeous day that David would have and should be enjoying on the river.

I played in the Philharmonic Children's Concerts in May but my heart felt dead. I felt like a robot while I played, utterly bereft of any emotion. I love classical music, but I couldn't listen to it because all of it sounded sad. For several years after David died, Christmas songs seemed melancholy, especially "I'll be Home for Christmas" and "Have Yourself a Merry Little Christmas." A line in the latter says, "through the years we all will be together, if the fates allow." I'd think, "The 'fates' didn't allow this for our family." (Nor did they allow it for the family of the young Karen Carpenter who sings the song).

Since I was depressed and couldn't enjoy anything, the evenings loomed before me. Emptiness washed over me and all I could do was lie on the floor and cry. One night I cried so hard I felt like I was choking and couldn't breathe. I panicked so badly that I called Jeanne and she came over to be with me. Another night I called a different friend and invited her to go out to dinner with me. Things do and did get better. Eventually a grieving person begins to concentrate more on the life of the loved one, rather than their death.

When I could read again, I immersed myself in books written by bereaved parents. One of the first ones I read was *Lament for a Son* by Nicholas Wolterstorff. I related to this father's pain because his young adult son was also an athlete who died pursuing an activity he loved--- mountain climbing.

Using the journal I received at the memorial service from David's supervisor, I began to record what I thought would be happy memories. Although I did include happy memories, initially I primarily wrote about my devastated emotional state. Reading it a year or two later, I saw how far I had come in my grief journey. It's tough to re-visit those first six months of deep pain, but it's therapeutic, as well.

Looking back at my journal now I notice an almost "frantic" social calendar that summer. Other people react by isolating; I was the opposite. If anyone wrote on a sympathy card "call me" or "let's get together," I took them up on it, whether I felt they really meant it or not. I arranged lunch or dinner with old friends and especially looked forward to getting together with David's friends. I called people and initiated the get together or accepted invitations as they came along. In a few of the sympathy cards people mentioned that they, or a good friend, had lost a child. Often these people also wrote down their phone numbers on the cards. I always followed up on these.

I sought out friends from my past who had lost a child. Some had lost children as much as 20 years ago--- true veterans of the bereaved parent "club." This is a club for which one does not wish to qualify. I called these people and boldly invited myself over to their homes to talk about how they had survived their ordeal.

I thought about David's friend, Charlie Beavers, who had died from an accident a couple of years earlier at age 21. I wanted to meet his parents but didn't know where they lived. About a year later I discovered that his mother lived in Spokane. I had to take a trip to Coeur d'Alene for work, so I asked if I could visit her. She kindly accepted, and I met her at her office. We cried and shared stories. Before leaving I noticed a photo on her bulletin board with 11 male kayakers from the Pyranha team, including David. Their manager, Dixie-Marree Prickett, was also in the photo. This was the photo taken at the memorial river run for Charlie in Steamboat Springs, June 2003. I thanked her when she gave me a copy. Sadly, within three years of that photo being taken, four of the team of 12, had died. Charlie died first, Matt Sheridan next, David next, then Daniel de la Vergne died in 2005. Out of those four, only one died in a kayaking incident. How shocking that one-fourth of the young men photographed died in such a brief time frame.

I posted a note about this photo on a kayak website and received several responses from people who knew one or more of these four young athletes. Dixie-Marree sent me an email describing an even more "eerie" photo she had seen of David, Daniel, Charlie, and Matt standing in front of Charlie's red truck in California. They were on their way to run Upper Cherry Creek, summer of 2002. She wrote:

> It gives me chills and is really unbelievable how life can change in the blink of an eye. I miss those boys so much and not a day goes by that I don't think about them. They all lived life to the fullest and followed their passions---and that is more than one can ask for. David was such a unique person. I loved his drive, passion, energy, and enthusiasm. I know you must miss him terribly but you probably have wonderful memories that keep you going. I think of them all together, having a blast running the most incredible rivers and looking down on us. I feel those boys with me all the time.

I so appreciate her and the others who have reached out to me over the years.

# Chapter 40

## David Projects

Not only was my social calendar frantic in those first few months after David died, but I also began a series of "David Projects," which continue to this day--- this story of his life being one of the major projects. At first I was afraid that as time passed I would forget David and forget what it was like to be his mother and to have him in my life. How I was blessed with the 52 hours of raw footage that he left behind! If he were to have willed anything of his material possessions, I think he would have known his film was his biggest legacy to us. Also he left about 600 slides from his pre-video camera days, so I'm sure they are of his early kayaking years. I bought a device recently that converts slides to scanned photos that can be put on the computer---yet another project awaits.

David was an avid writer and journalist. Considering that he really didn't like to read and didn't care for school that much, I commented to him once about how he liked to write. He brushed that comment aside with, "I have to make a living." However he did journal from early on as I found out after he died; he left me precious insights into his life and adventures that I cherish.

During the first month after David died I typed up a detailed ten-page outline of highlights of his life, hoping to write a book about him when I retired. Later I found a journal I had written when Amy and David were in elementary school. It brought back memories of humorous incidents that I had forgotten. I knew David had written a brief outline of his life as well, covering the highlights of his career from age 18- 24. He titled it: "Life begins at 18." This has proven to be very helpful in writing this book. How ironic it seems that the night before he died, David updated his bio with new information regarding his life up to the very last minute. Considering how busy he was that night---getting ready for the race and working on articles that were due in two days--- the fact that he took the time to do this seems, at the very least, eerie.

David wrote that in recent months, he'd become weekend editor at KTVB, signed on with new sponsors, and was feeling more welcome at new places. He'd also appeared on the cover of *Rapid Magazine*, hosted a premier of his video, and he'd met Lindsey.

I found next to his bio, a partial list of his short and long term goals for 2004. He wanted to build his resume and increase his business by networking, win the IR Big Gun contest again, sell more TV footage and publish more articles, land another cover shot on a major magazine, secure a position as cameraman on *The Apprentice*, and he wanted to extensively video tape and photograph in Idaho. He had his eye on several kayaking missions, particularly in BC. He summed up with "be strong in negotiations; don't leave feeling beaten." David met many of these goals in the four months that he was alive in 2004.

A small photo album was one of the earlier and easier projects I took on. Fortunately I kept photo albums most of my adult life so I just re-arranged some of them to make a special one of David and his friends. I drove around town taking pictures of all the places he lived as well as all of his schools. I made a scrapbook of events and articles written about him the week after he died.

Another early project was to find his video *The North Stein Experience* that he had shared with me the month before he died. I couldn't find it. I was delighted when Skip found it on David's computer and converted it to DVD for me.

One of the biggest projects I tackled , besides writing this book, was to compile a notebook of all the articles that appeared in the media about David over the years. Fortunately I had a large stack of the magazines in which I knew he had been published. Included in these were photos and articles written about him, and his own published photos and articles. There were some articles I didn't have and it took a few months to locate those on the internet. I learned about these from David's resumes. Between the years of 2000-2010 there were approximately 70 pieces (that I know of) written about him or by him. Seventeen of those were written posthumously.

Some of the magazines and newspapers he appeared in were *Kayak Magazine, Paddler, Rapid, American Whitewater, Canoe and Kayak, Kayak Session, Banks Magazine, Boise Weekly*, and *The Idaho Statesman*. In addition when he was 11, he was quoted in *The Idaho Statesman* after they had interviewed several people who were watching a school fire that Christmas Eve. I made copies of all the articles and their magazine covers and put them in sheet protectors. I also included his unpublished articles, which were a great help to me in compiling some of the adventures for this book.

Shortly after David died someone called from Spike TV asking to talk to David. When I informed the man that he had died, he expressed his surprise and condolences. He told me David had recently sent them film and talked to them about the possibility of selling some of his footage for one of their shows, about wild and crazy sport-type antics. They no longer had the film but were interested in reviewing it again, especially his urban kayaking footage. After I found the footage and mailed it to them, they responded with a desire to purchase the film for use in one of their productions. The show aired several times.

Over the next couple of years I was approached by other networks and entertainment companies who were interested in reviewing David's footage. This prompted one of my next projects which was cataloguing his 52 hours of video. David had catalogued it by labeling what each one-hour segment of film was about. He had made half a dozen six-hour long VHS compilations of his 52 mini-DV film cassettes; these were compiled by the year in which the material was filmed. Shortly after he died I bought a DVD/VHS player that converted VHS to DVD. I converted all of these to DVD so they would last longer. I watched them all and took notes about what was in each one. The networks always wanted the original film so I reviewed all of those in an attempt to catalog them as well.

I feel so blessed with all the film of David and his friends. I think of people who lost a child before the advent of photography or those who only had a couple of photos of their child. I am lucky to have David's voice, his movements, his laugh, and his silly antics to keep his memory fresh, vivid, and close to my heart.

Revising David's website, **www.therevolution.cc**, was another of my projects. His webmaster, Skip, helped me. I first announced his death on page one, and thanked everyone for all their support to our family during that time. Then I added more photos of his life, some of his personal writings, and best of all, adventures and tributes his friends had written about him.

About a year after David died, Donelle Lee, a high school friend of his, called me. She asked me what was the cause of David's death as she had a young son with a heart defect. She also shared a dream about David that she had shortly after he passed. She was standing in line at a grocery store and David turned around and said, "Hi." He told her he was going to be in a race the next day. She pleaded, "No David! Don't go!" He said, "That's okay, I'll be fine." Then they hugged. I really appreciate friends telling me dreams they have about David; I write them down along with the dreams I have about him. I believe if there is a way those on the other side can attempt to communicate with us, it might be through our dreams. Donelle introduced me to MySpace and I began a three-year blog with stories about David's life as well as writing about my own grief journey.

Another on-going project is reviewing David's computer files. There is always something new to discover. Needless to say I've become more electronically savvy since he died. He used to tease me about my limited computer skills, so I hope he would be proud of me. I came across a contest he had entered at my suggestion, although I had never seen his entry until after he died. Mervyns was offering an all-expenses paid family reunion trip to San Diego for

Mother's Day. The entrants had to write about what makes their mother great. David wrote:

> What makes my mother wonderful is her gracious support and willingness to help me out wherever I may be headed in life. Emotionally and physically she is there to help guide me through this ever-changing journey that is life. She continues to live her life as fully as she wants while enjoying life's simple pleasures. I also love to see her be an amazing, caring grandmother, giving guidance to my sister and her daughter as they go through the same challenges as Mom did raising my sister and me. So much parental knowledge she has to pass on.

Something new and interesting is revealed each time I browse through David's computer files, which as of this date I've not completed. For example, here is part of a letter he wrote to his sister, Amy, two months before he died, referencing his 16-month old niece:

> I bet Anna is really trouble now. Getting to know her own voice and using new words. I really wish I could see her right now. I'm missing a very important time in her life. Hopefully this summer I will be able to see her. I need to so that she doesn't forget who I am or lose me from her vocabulary.

This breaks my heart each time I read it. It feels like pre-cognition about what was about to happen to him. I am determined to keep the memory of Uncle David alive for his niece and nephews. A few months after David died, I made a storybook about him for Anna with pictures of David and her. I share his adventures with nephews, Josef and Ben---born after he died. They love watching his kayak videos.

Of course this book has been the biggest project in my endeavor to keep David's memory alive. All the time I spent compiling and cataloguing his published and non-published writings, journal, and raw footage helped me immensely in putting together this book. Writing it has been a blessing to me. It has brought me closer to David's many friends as well.

# Chapter 41

## In Remembrance of Dave

As I've mentioned, one of the things that held me together during that summer of 2004 was being around David's friends: Lindsey, Kasia, Graham, Kelli, Dan, Dru and his family, Tara, Roger, Betsy, Sara and Shannon Thun , Donelle, Byl, Aaron , Matt, the Eschens, Richard, Skip, Joe, Tyler, Dustin, Brad, Will, Brent, Ryan, and so many others. I knew they wouldn't always be around Boise so we decided to host a barbecue for his friends. I was so thankful Amy and Travis were able to be there as well. We held our first "annual" barbecue on July 9, 2004, with several others to follow in the next few summers.

I busied myself making memory packets. These contained at least one DVD, usually the *Idaho Whitewater Wrap Up*, some photos, an article or two, a bumper sticker--- either the "Do It for Dave" and/or *Broke Hungry and Happy*, along with his personal essay, "The Daily Grind." I mailed memory packets to those friends who lived too far away to make it to the barbecue.

Thanks to all the friends, food and beer flowed abundantly, as did memories of happy times. We showed one of David's DVDs and I handed out the memory packets. I invited anyone who wanted other DVDs to ask me; I would burn copies and mail them. Everyone cheered and thanked Mike and me for hosting a great party. I provided a notebook to record everyone's address and phone number along with a brief note about how they met David or some other story. What follows is a rich sample of some of the stories David's friends shared:

Byl Kravetz told how they met and said, "Thanks for the good times, Dave."

Lindsey wrote about how they met, being introduced by a friend, and "that was that." She said during spring break she was sick and David came over to take care of her. He tried to make her eat a clove of garlic, and she said, "No way! I would rather be sick."

Brad Baccus wrote:

> I met Dave on the North Fork when he had a full face mask football helmet. He swam and looked shady, but became one of the best paddlers in Idaho. We all need to keep coming together for events to celebrate his life.

Dru described his recollections of meeting David the first time:

> I took notice of Dave right away. Keep in mind this is back in the early days of kayaking, before the days of the planing hull even. Your typical kayaker was more the granola eating, hacky sack kicking type than a tattoo sporting, studded punk rock belt holding up military cargoes cutoff into shorts type of person. Dave was cruising the Otter Slide campground parking lot on an old BMX bike. Instantly I wished I had one too. In what I would come to know as common Dangerous Dave style, he stood out by simply doing his own thing his own way. Dave wore glasses, and even though he used to wear these ridiculous racquetball goggles when he was boating, he looked so cool, I wished I knew him. I wanted to hang out with him, wanted him for a friend. Funny how things work out sometimes.

Brent Peterson talked about how they met at a rodeo in Bend, Oregon. "He was one of the best; Dave has inspired me to push my kayaking."

Christian and Nikola Eschen wrote:

> We remember Dave's kindness and good natured 'let's go boating' attitude. We remember the fun brother we could always count on to get Christian to try one more ride. He was

a young man who always had a smile and word of encouragement and thanks for the day we were given.

Shannon Thun wrote:

> Having met Dave through Dan Menten, I was struck the most by his admiration and will power to never settle for anything but the best and extreme.

Tara Sanders who met David's sister Amy at high school wrote:

> When I'd be around Dave at the Payettes, I immediately felt very sisterly towards him. I felt as if I was part of his family. I had the chance to see 'little Dave' away from home and out in the world. Seeing Dave always gave me a little taste of home, but home is where the heart is. I miss him and love him.

Will Parham who only met Dave a few weeks before he died wrote:

> I met Dave at Climax Wave (on the Payette River). He was so friendly; he made kayaking fun with his excessive energy. I was honored to be paddling with him. I had previously only admired him in his videos. He told me that I reminded him of himself when he was younger. I really look up to Dave. I hope I can be as influential as he was. I hope to be as happy and make people as happy as he did.

*\*\*\**

Graham Wright and Kelli Jeffress were a constant at the barbecues and in my life. David in fact had introduced them a couple of years before he died, and as of the writing of this book they have grown into a sweet family with two young girls. I'm sure David would be pleased how his match making turned out. When I interviewed Graham for this book, he shared openly some of his thoughts about his friendship with David. He said:

> Dave could be off-putting, cocky, arrogant, full of himself. Dave probably thought I was arrogant too, but somehow we met in the middle and forged a great friendship. Once I got to know the "true" Dave, I found he was the most genuine person who would do anything for you. I was a protégé of Dave; he mentored me along in my kayaking,

instilling confidence in me. We paddled little boats in big water down the North Fork, and sometimes I was scared. He taught me good hand signals, how to be safe, how to keep my cool. When there were life-threatening situations, there was no one I'd rather have my back than Dave. I feel I'm a "Dave-like" paddler now. In addition to Matt Elam, Dru, Dan, Jim Grossman, Dave Simonitis, the Bear Valley crew, and many other kayakers, we kayaked with three friends who have since passed away: Russell Kelly, Damon Miller, and Conrad Fourney.

Dave was also a very talented snow boarder; we boarded two seasons at Bogus Basin together. He knew the mountain like the back of his hand. He boarded like he kayaked; he was an acrobat, doing front flips and other stunts. He even tried to get me to eat better: sprouts, good deli-type sandwiches, no burgers and fries. I miss him a lot.

I appreciate the story that Kelli wrote in 2004 about David, and read at the YMCA Heritage dinner that year. She describes his race:

On April 24, 2004 , after kayaking down the Boise River, David set out on his bike to climb hundreds of feet in elevation up Bogus Basin Road. He passed many friends along the way with a smile. On that day Dave's journey would take him farther than the peaks of Bogus. David rode his bike off this earth and out of our world, to heaven. Time stood still. Everyone who Dave touched in his 24 years on this earth was forever changed. We all stood in utter shock and disbelief. David lived a full life, more than some men live who live three times as long as he did. He packed so much into his 24 years.

Obviously David's friends being kayakers were all over the world and are not always in Boise when we had barbecues. Many have written me sweet emails about what David meant to them, and these mean so much to me. Chad Crabtree, who was in Durango with David and also on the Costa Rica trip told me:

David was an incredible person and paddler, and he is on my mind every time I'm on the river. Ever since Toby (Scarpella) died, I seem to see a butterfly or two no matter where I am or which creek or river it is. I like to think they are Dave, Toby, Charlie B. and the rest of my fallen friends that are watching over me while paddling.

Although Joe Carberry wasn't able to be at the barbecue since he had moved to another state, he wrote to me the following, which touched me:

> Dave pushed the envelope. He set bars for himself and continually strived to his wits end to complete his personal projects. It was something I've always admired about him. I also watched him mature from an insecure young kid to a promising young man, learning to edit video and creating a niche for himself that could have taken him wherever he wanted to go. I remember visiting him at his basement apartment, listening to his plans, impressed with his ideas and rooting like hell for him to succeed. He didn't need any encouragement. He was a driven, smart soul with loads of talent. I was completely devastated [when he died]. Dave carved an indelible place in whitewater. Keep the faith, Rae Ann. The world is better, for me, because Dave lived in it. Even if his time was too short.

Nikki Kelly, world class kayaker later wrote to me: "I feel fortunate to have spent some time with David. Be assured that he lived a rich life, an inspiration for all of us to make the most of every moment."

Erik Boomer, another top-notch kayaker, wrote to me:

> I'd seen David in magazines and movies for a few years and looked up to him a lot. He came to McCall/Riggins and we paddled for about a week, surfing Gold's Hole. He had tons of energy and never seemed to wear out. Then we paddled a creek which was new to me at that time. He pushed me to try it. We came to a portage; I pulled over in the pool above and said, "We portage here, right?" He said, "I see an eddy just above the log jam." He paddled through the entrance, caught the eddy, and looked back at me to see what I would do. I paddled down to him and we ended having to hike back up and portage at the original spot anyway. We hiked up Hazard Creek five miles to see a falls. On the way down we were talking about planning for later in life, and he was very adamant, saying, "You don't know if you will even

be alive when you're older, you may as well make every day the best and live in the moment." From what I could see he stuffed a couple lifetimes into his 24 years. He may have gotten flack for living broke, hungry and happy, but he definitely was not storing up treasures here on earth that he could not take with him.

Corey Volt later told me how he heard that David had died. Corey had been kayaking in California and was hitchhiking to Oregon when he received a phone call from his mother. She had read an article about David's death in the Ogden paper and called Corey. It was only a couple of hours before David's memorial service so Corey was unable to get there in time. He was deeply saddened. He told me to this day he thinks of Dave often and it offers him the motivation to strive for great things. Corey continues to love the sport as he kayaks all over the world.

I cherish all the kind thoughts and memories that his friends have shared with me over the years. During the next few summers we had other barbecues and continued to meet "new" friends. It has always been a blessing.

*\*\**

After the memorial I couldn't bear the thought of bringing David's ashes to the house so I asked the funeral home to keep them for awhile. Two months later, I thought, "What am I thinking? Why should David's ashes be in a stranger's house, a business, instead of with me? It's time to bring him home."

I told my boss what I was doing and that I would be an hour late or so. I ended up being three hours late to work as it was even tougher than I had imagined. I cried all the way to the funeral home and all the way back home. Then I crawled into bed and wept. But it felt right to have David "home."

Recalling Charlie Beavers' river memorial during which his ashes were released into one of his favorite rivers, I thought something like this would be a loving tribute to my son. David's friends could take some of his ashes and sprinkle them in Climax Wave, one of his favorite play spots on the Payette River north of Horseshoe Bend.

Earlier I commissioned a local artist to design two small, yellow ceramic kayaks in which to save some of the ashes. The funeral home placed ashes in each of these boats and split the remainder into two containers; one to be buried with me and the other to be released in Climax Wave. I gave Amy one of the boats and kept one for myself. Mine is in the living room on top of a bookcase along with a piece of wood and some dried flowers from the place on Bogus Basin Road where David died.

*** 

On July 9, 2005 Mike and I, Amy, Travis, Anna (3 years old), Josef (7 month old), Dru, and Lindsey drove to Climax for a ceremony. We were there to remember and honor our beloved son, brother, uncle, best friend, and boyfriend. We gathered in a circle by the wave; Mike recited the 23rd Psalm and said a prayer. We shared more memories of David. Dru , tearful and quiet, finally looked at the sky and yelled , "Dave my friend, hear me! Our spirits are with your spirit. I love you and miss you." To this day it breaks my heart to see how much David's best friends miss him and how much it broke their hearts to lose him. I hope and believe that David was with us that day.

Dru put on David's life jacket, took David's ashes with him in his kayak, and paddled into the center of the wave where he released the ashes. Then Dru impressed us with some tricky kayak maneuvers in the wave while we cheered him on. Amy, Mike, Lindsey, and I threw flowers into the wave. It was a sad occasion, yet uplifting for me. We were also buoyed by the prospect of the 2nd Annual Friends of Dave Norell Barbecue, which we were hosting that evening.

The following year David's sweet dog Jenny died; I took her ashes to the same wave, and sprinkled them on the shore. She used to love running gleefully up and down the shore watching David kayak.

# Chapter 42

## Forging Strength out of Adversity

A couple of weeks after David died I felt I needed to get some help with my grief. Being a social worker, I figured there must be a group for bereaved parents. One of the local hospitals provided me with the phone number for The Compassionate Friends. When I called TCF and explained that my son had just died, they told me about their monthly support group. I attended my first meeting just three weeks after David died. I walked in alone and was confronted with a room full of parents like me. A shock wave enveloped me when I realized why I qualified to be a member of this group; I started to cry and walk out. Fortunately someone talked to me, and I agreed to stay.

The meeting started with each parent telling the name of their child, his or her age, and how they had died. I heard stories from stillbirth, to suicide, accidental gunshot wound, drowning, automobile accidents, long term illness, sudden illness, etc. It was overwhelming, but whatever the ages or manner of death, we held a common bond; each of us mourned the loss of a beloved child. It was so overwhelming that I almost didn't return the following month, but something drew me back. It was the chance to talk freely about our children. Often, a few weeks after the death of a child or loved one, no one wants to mention the deceased's name for fear we will cry; or they think, "You should be over this by now." At TCF people understood. They were not likely to say something trite like, "He/she is in a better place now," or "It was God's will," or "You can have other children."

After one year of participating in TCF I was asked to assume leadership of the group. It's facilitated by lay people rather than professionals, although I happened to be a licensed clinical social worker. My duties include organizing the program, finding and recruiting new facilitators, and facilitating some of the meetings. Fortunately there are several other strong leaders on the steering committee so I have lots of help. Attending some of the national TCF conferences around the country has been a blessing to me. In helping others, I help myself. This is how I developed strength through the sorrow of my great loss.

Another group I found on the internet is Parent Heart Watch. I submitted David's story with a photo and they were posted. This is a group for parents who have a child living with a congenital heart condition, or who have lost a child to a heart condition. It's not uncommon for children to die suddenly due to an undiagnosed congenital heart defect. The mission of PHW is to educate the medical community and schools, particularly the sports programs about the importance of thorough medical screenings before children engage in competitive sports. Many of the chapters have been successful in getting legislation passed in their states to require AEDs in their schools and at sporting events.

My time is limited and because I chose to be active in The Compassionate Friends, I am not active in Parent Heart Watch. However, two years after David died I was contacted by an organization affiliated with PHW that presented me with an AED to give to a school. When I donated the AED to David's school, Capital High, I told the principal the history of David's fainting during wrestling. Because Capital is such a big school, the principal was pleased to add another AED to their safety equipment. He told me he would have a plaque made with David's name on it to hang in the gymnasium by the AED.

# Chapter 43

### The Legend of Dangerous Dave

As happens when someone dies young, various "legends" often grow about that person. David was dubbed "Dangerous Dave" early on, well before he passed. There are numerous theories as to how he got that label; I'd like to share a few. I know why David got the title, because he told me. I also found it in his writings after he died. However, these other stories would have qualified him for that moniker as well.

As Dan Menten suggested, some would say David's adventurous nature was genetic, that he inherited it from his dad, who was infamous in the early days on the Payette River. As mentioned before, Mike suffered repetitive beatings at Mike's Hole on the Payette, and David also got worked on various rivers. Aside from David's vivacious attitude and aggressively youthful personality, he was just a dangerous guy.

In their earliest video *Gardena Derby* there were crash and burn segments showing David doing many cartwheels. He took a log to the chest on Hazard Creek, and ran class V rapids upside-down at an early age. However, as Dan and Dru later attested, he was methodical and calculating, scouting and portaging when he thought some stretch of water was beyond his ability.

David told me he got his nickname from his driving. One time he was with Dru and they were in a hurry to paddle the Payettes. When approaching the bottom of the notorious Horseshoe Bend Hill, there was only 100 feet or so of passing lane left and three cars were in front of him. David gunned it to about 90 miles per hour in his little "sketch-mobile" and passed two of the cars after the lane ended. Then he had to slow down immediately for the town of Horseshoe Bend. David admitted he also got the title, secondarily, for some close calls on the river.

As a mother, the driving stories scared me more than the kayaking stories. Many a night before David would take off on his trips, I prayed for a band of angels to not only surround his kayak at all times on the river, but to surround his car as he drove, often all night after a full day of kayaking. During the interview in my home, two days after David died, I told Channel 6: "I pray daily for both my children, but I never expected David to die on a bicycle." Today as I write this I'm struck with and saddened by the fact that I didn't specifically pray for a band of angels to surround his bicycle on the race that day.

A bit of mystery or legend if you will, surrounds the OIL phenomena. However, I'm sworn to secrecy as to how and why David and his good friends Tyler, Dru, Dan, and Dustin came up with this. "OIL" upside down and backwards, as David and his friends pointed out, looks like the number "710." We can celebrate David's life every year at precisely 7:10 a.m. and/or 7:10 p.m. on July 10 (7/10) by doing something silly such as headstands, somersaulting down the hall, or anything--- limited only by the imagination. Tyler often calls me on 7/10 at 7:10 to wish me well and to reminisce about David with me.

There can't be a book about David without some discussion of his relationship with money. Although this does not relate to how he got the nickname Dangerous Dave, a type of legend has grown around his use of money. Some would say David was a tight wad, or that he did not want to part with his money. I would say that David was simply passionate about being able to kayak; kayaking takes both a lot of money and a lot of time on the road, making it difficult to earn enough in a few short months each year. Because David wasn't a "trust fund baby" as he once lamented to me, he worked long and hard during the few winter months he wasn't kayaking full-time to earn and save all he could for the kayak season. His kayak season was longer than his winter months, as you could often find David kayaking the Payette in February.

As I mentioned earlier, I found out after he died that he had three dollars in checking, a few thousand in savings, and an IRA with $2000. He had a truck that was free and clear and no other bills. He knew how to save on rent and on the road.

David rode his bike around town whenever possible to save money on gas. He thought it was exorbitant when gas prices topped two dollars per gallon in 2004. What might he have thought when gasoline rose to $3.95 per gallon in Boise?

David planned and budgeted, often coming home from a long trip with only one dollar to spare. I tried to get him to take a credit card for emergencies on road trips, but he was loath to use a credit card. When he did charge something, he paid it off the following month. David had more money saving tricks up his sleeve. He knew friends who worked at a local pizza place who gave him free pizza on Tuesdays. His friends Graham and Kelli claimed he had a second sense about when they were having pizza and would show up at their house just in time. He'd survive on Ramen and bologna without bread. He loved his weekly free lunches dining with me; I didn't mind as I enjoyed his company. His friend Dru said he knew how to work a room in a bar. He'd sit down with strangers, join in on a lively conversation and end up being offered beer. His ability to "schmooze" free beer notwithstanding, he once wrote: "Beer is a large drain on the budget. It is *not* essential!"

David also earned money from the many articles he wrote for publication. He actually wrote an article, as yet unpublished, about this very topic--- how to make and save money and how to make the dollars stretch during kayak season. He wrote: "You only need three essentials to kayak: gear, gas and grub. The gear lets you kayak, the gas gets you to the kayaking, and the grub powers the kayak. Some other tips: put all money earned in savings right away, don't carry much cash, do invest in an IRA. Work hard, play hard, because you only live once."

# Chapter 44

## David's Blessings to Us

*Blessed are they that mourn for they shall be comforted.*
*Matt. 5:4*

David left us many blessings. I have indeed been comforted especially by David's friends and colleagues, many of whom have stayed in touch with me over the years. Through Facebook I keep up with David's friends and their adventures: kayaking, traveling, marriages, children. Since David died, I've met friends and contacts of his I never knew about. So many have blessed me by sharing their stories about David. Without these friends I would not have been able to write the middle portion of this book, the story of my son's many kayaking trips and adventures.

I'm touched by what David's good friend Dan Menten wrote to me about a year after David died:

> It was routine to be on a creek with Dave and upon arriving at some heinous looking rapid hear him declare, "It looks good!" His greatest values were hard work, determination, and the fulfillment of his goals as a paddler. He accomplished so much in a very short time; it was his own internal clock that would inevitably dictate this urgency. Paddling is an intrinsically mental sport that requires focus, concentration, and memory to be performed safely. Finding this balance between risk and comfort is a lesson we must

continuously learn. Risking injury as well as having the required ability and focus to paddle class V whitewater is as much a lifestyle as it is a sport. Dave's passion for life was unmatched: living for today and regretting nothing tomorrow, he lived according to humble and realistic wants and unique and minimalist needs. If he had known about his heart condition and had to curtail his involvement in kayaking and other sports, it would have terminally compromised his happiness. He was an adventurer and lover of the hard work entailed in outdoors and wilderness pursuits. To love your life so much that you follow your dreams is the lesson that we can all take seriously. His happiness reverberates in so many people. Live the life you want, not the life you're told--- Do It for Dave.

Famed kayaker and kayak film producer, Scott Lindgren, shared these thoughts about David with me:

David was well on his way to making those subtle changes that would have propelled him to the next level in the kayak film industry. He managed to show me and many others that he had the ability to survive. There is nothing more powerful than a river. It is a mind, body, balance sport that requires an insane amount of focus. It incorporates every component of life every time you are on the water. You will only find a handful of people in the world that operate at David's level. I'm sorry that David never got the opportunity to show the world his maximum potential. He did prove to the core community that he was someone to be respected. David was living life to the fullest. What more can any of us ask for? For me, nothing, because that is how I have lived my life.

Another blessing is David's continued appearance in the media: TV, newspapers, books, magazines, new DVDs. There is a page about his 70-foot drop at Bear Creek written by Joe Carberry in the book *Idaho Paddler* that was published in 2009. He was also featured going over this fall on the DVD that accompanies the book. Some of his footage also appeared in a video that Trey Chace produced called *The White Album*.

I had been thinking about the teasers David made a couple months before he died, *Idaho Whitewater Wrap Up*, and his North Stein film. Some sponsorships for David's new video had fallen through shortly before he died. David had commented: "It's a shame that I have so much fantastic footage that no one will get to see." In 2008 it dawned on me: "Why shouldn't people be able to see this footage?" I contacted Eric Link, producer of the *Twitch* series David appeared in, to ask him if he would be interested in some of David's footage. Eric and Tao Berman were both enthusiastic about using some of David's unpublished video in their upcoming film *Pulse*.

On April 9, 2008 *Pulse* premiered in Boise. The owners of Inland Surf, who were sponsoring the event, invited me to tell the story of how David's footage made its way into this DVD. The room was packed with kayaking enthusiasts. Eric had artfully edited David's film. A chapter entitled *The Revolution III* was devoted to David's footage. Included were several scenes of David's plunge over the huge waterfall at Bear Creek, set to music that really touched me. Eric was hesitant about the "epitaph" at the end, but I encouraged him to use it. After the showing that night at Inland Surf, the crowd cheered.

## David Norell

**Punk kid who**
**Loved whitewater.**

**He got its message**
**And understood.**

**You couldn't help**
**But love him for that.**

**He left early.**

**Viva la Revolucion! [16]**

*I* think David should have lived to 50, 60, 75, but he didn't. However, his life spanned four decades. He was born in 1979, thus he lived in the 70's, 80's, 90's and the first decade of the "2000's". It makes him sound so much older when I think of it in these terms and helps me come to grips with the brevity of his life. David lived to be a quarter of a century old, dying 28 days before his 25th birthday. Not only did he witness the ushering in of a new century, but a new millennium as well! I am blessed to have known him as a young man well on his way to an established career. He could have died in the first year or two of his life, or at age 10, due to his heart condition, but he didn't. Relationships between parents and their grown children are so rewarding; I'm grateful David and I shared this together.

At times I have gotten deep into a pity party over *my* loss---a mother's loss---the loss of an only son---after all a parent is supposed to leave this earth before their child. Whenever I find myself going down this dark path I remind myself it's not *my* loss that is so heavy. David suffered the deepest loss. He is the one who left this earth too soon, not me. I know he'd rather be here kayaking and having adventures with his friends. I envision him kayaking with his friends who have gone on as well, in some huge whitewater rivers on the other side.

I decorated my office walls with several posters and photos of David plunging down waterfalls or standing on terra firma, grinning from ear to ear. The waterfall photos especially sparked conversations with people, even those who didn't know David. It gave me an opportunity to share a little about his exciting life. I'm not shy; I always bragged about my daughter, my son, and my grandchildren as well. I continue to brag about David even though he is not here with us. We keep our loved ones' memories alive by saying their names.

Shortly after David died I heard a song on the radio sung by Tim McGraw, "Live Like you were Dying." It reminded me of David. It's about a man who found out he had a terminal illness and only had a few months to live. He was asked, "What did you do when you found out the news?" He said, "I went sky diving, I went rocky mountain climbing, I went bull riding. I forgave deeper, spent more time with loved ones," etc. He said, "Someday I hope you'll get the chance to live like you were dying."

I thought, David traveled the world, kayaked class V and VI whitewater, saw God's beautiful scenery, had many friends, went sky diving, hot air ballooning, bungee jumping, snowboarding, parachuting, caving in the dark, and other things I'm sure I'm not aware of. He truly lived squeezing in every exciting moment he could throughout his life. This quote of unknown origin, reminds me of how David lived: "Life is not a journey to the grave with the intention of arriving safely with a well preserved body, but rather to slide in broadside, totally worn out, loudly proclaiming, *Whew!* What a ride!"

I consider myself a wimp, and I think David might have agreed. I like to read, write, knit, watch movies, walk, travel ---generally do "safe" things. However, I decided when David died to follow his example and try some more exciting things that to me had a bit of risk involved. No, I'm not taking up kayaking! I certainly know my limits. I'm no stranger to travel. At 20, I traveled all over Europe for two months by myself. I've since been to Ireland, Jamaica, France, all over the US, Mexico, and Canada. But since David died, I've been to Hawaii, England, to France again, and explored more adventurous terrain such as China, Peru, and Egypt. I hope to get to Costa Rica soon to see the beautiful country where David kayaked.

Since David died I've also rafted the South Fork of the Payette and been snowmobiling. (Granted I was nervous.) I took up motorcycle riding, as a passenger that is. Howard and I have put many miles on our Honda Goldwing. In 2008 we took a trip to southwestern Colorado, traveling to Telluride, Ouray, Durango, and other places. While in Durango I used the time to visit Ft. Lewis College, including the dorm room that David lived in for one semester, and a house he shared with Skip Armstrong and other friends.

In 2009 Howard and I took the Goldwing through parts of British Columbia and Alberta. David loved this part of Canada; it is such a beautiful place. Best of all I got to meet a couple of his good

Canadian kayaking friends, Karla Suderland and Corey Boux. In 2010 we traveled by motorcycle to the Oregon Coast and northern California. We visited Dan Menten in Trinidad and Andrew West in Grass Valley. It was so good to see them again and to get their invaluable input for the book. I like to think that David would be amazed and pleased that his wimpy mom is having exciting motorcycle adventures.

In retrospect, David helped me realize that pursuing one's dreams is more important than following the expectations of your heritage. Since my paternal grandfather graduated from University of Purdue as an engineer, higher education has been a cornerstone of my family. I'm thankful David didn't complete four years of college. He would have been spending one third of his life following our dream for him, not his dream. David's message to us was to live life to the fullest, don't waste a moment, and do the things you love. Set goals and go about achieving them. There are times you may fail, but persevere and you'll find another way to achieve your dreams. I'm sure David would have agreed with Mark Twain, who said:

> Twenty years from now you will be more disappointed by the things you didn't do than the things you did do. So throw off the bowlines, sail away from the safe harbor. Catch the trade winds in your sails. Explore. Dream. Discover.

To paraphrase a song called "The Comet" that I heard in Dearborn, Michigan at the national convention of The Compassionate Friends, David's life was like a comet. He streaked across our sky with a brilliant light, but was gone in an instant. We watched in awe and wonder at what this comet had done. While we watched his journey, how could we have known his time on earth would be so short? We can only search for answers in the life he lived. We thank him for sharing his light, his inspiration. We will carry on the best we can and share his dreams and aspirations. We thank him for the time he spent with us and the passion he shared with us. "We won't forget your comet light until the end of time." [17]

Ironically a couple of years before David died, he put this "epitaph" on his website and in his video *Broke, Hungry and Happy*: "The loss of a kayaking soul is always tough. But we must persist on. True feelings and emotions between comrades shine through in this grand finale." I recently bought a small plaque and placed it next to a photo of David plunging over a waterfall. It states: "Life is not measured by the number of breaths we take, but by the moments that take our breath away." Although he was way too young when he left us, I find comfort in knowing David lived an exciting life, doing what he loved. He had so many moments that surely took his breath away. For this I am forever grateful.

David we love you and we will never forget you.

# The End

# Whitewater Terminology

(Re-produced in part with permission from Wetdawg.com)

1. **Boil:** Swirly or unpredictable currents pushing (boiling) to the surface. Usually caused by currents rebounding off the river bed, pushing the water to the surface.
2. **Boof:** A technique used to drive your kayak for a mini-launch over a shallow ledge or rock. This move can help propel your kayak over the hole formed at the bottom of the drop.
3. **C.F.S. (cfs):** Cubic Feet per Second. A standard measurement of velocity of water flow at a given point in a river which measures how many cubic feet of water pass that specific point in one second. This will vary according to water level and the gradient of the riverbed.
4. **Carnage:** A general term for accidents on the river. Often involves bodily injury, blood.
5. **Confluence:** Where two or more forks of a river, or two separate rivers flow into each other.
6. **Creek:** A small river, usually run by expert boaters when flowing at high water. Almost always has lots of holes, logs ("wood"), drops, etc. (creeking)
7. **Drop:** A short, steep rapid or section of a rapid. Named for the abrupt increase in gradient between the top and bottom of the rapid.
8. **Eddy:** A place in a river where the water is moving in a different direction or different speed than the main current. Eddies are made by rocks in the river, outcroppings along the side, behind logs, bridge pilings, and also in the inside of bends or along the side of the river. Eddies are places where kayakers can sit and stay relatively still instead of floating downstream. They come in handy for scouting, resting, accessing play spots, etc.
9. **Eddy Hop:** To run a rapid in stages by catching the eddies as you go down. For some rapids, it's a good way to scout.

10. **Eddy Line:** The part of a river that separates an eddy from the main current. They can range from gentle changes of current, to violent, whirl-pool-causing obstacles. The speed, volume, and gradient of the current will decide what type of eddy line is formed.

11. **Ender:** Usually a play maneuver performed by burying a boats bow down and deep under water while the stern pops up. This results in a vertical position, and sometimes over-vertical.

12. **FPM:** Feet Per Mile: Used to describe a river's gradient by how many feet the river drops in one mile.

13. **Gnar, gnarly, the gnar:** extremely difficult and committing whitewater with oddly placed rocks and/or features such that passage requires precise movement. See also: Mank, Burl. (provided by Dan Menten).

14. **Gradient:** The steepness of a river over a specified distance, typically expressed in feet per mile (FPM). You can combine gradient and river flow information to make a generalization as to the difficulty and character of a particular run. Ex: Low-Volume Steep Creek (300 CFS, 200 FPM) or a mellow, high-volume run (10,000 CFS, 10 FPM).

15. **Hair:** Boater slang for extreme conditions with dangerous and difficult water. Hair Boating: Paddling in those conditions.

16. **Haystacks:** Very large, tall standing waves that tend to collapse chaotically near the crest of the wave. Typically a high-volume river feature.

17. **Hole:** Holes are formed from water pouring over a rock, ledge, or the obstacle in the river. The water directly behind the hole, called backwash, is fed back upstream to the hole, while the water underneath the hole, called outflow, will flush downstream.

18. **Horizon Line:** From the vantage point of your kayak, a horizon line will appear as a significant drop. When you can't see where the water goes, eddy out to scout the section you can't see from your kayak on shore.

19. **Hydraulic:** Refers to a water formation following a sudden drop in the riverbed or drop over an obstruction that creates a powerful re-circulating force at the base of a drop (hole). The circulating pressure of a powerful hydraulic can potentially hold boats and paddlers for indeterminate lengths of time depending on its size and strength.

20. **Loops**: A playboating move involving a vertical somersault where both ends of the boat engage in the hole without having your boat on edge.

21. **Nar:** see gnar

22. **Pin:** Being stuck in your kayak between the current and the river bed or an obstruction such as a rock or log. Pins are potentially deadly situations that may require a complex rescue.

23. **Portage:** Carrying boats around a difficult rapid or other obstructions.

24. **Put-in:** Starting place of a river trip, where you put your boat in the river to begin a run or trip.

25. **Reading Water:** Being able to see common aspects of river rapids, i.e. Current lines, rocks, clear channels, eddy lines, etc. By recognizing these things paddlers will be able to choose the safest path for their boat.

26. **River Left:** The left-hand side of the river when looking downstream. This is what most paddlers mean when indicating left---always think in terms of facing downstream.

27. **River Right:** The right-hand side of the river when looking downstream.

28. **River Mile:** Refers to a distance in miles from the mouth of the river.

29. **Roll:** The move performed to right a capsized kayak. It is accomplished with a paddle stroke and hip-snap.

30. **Seal Launch:** Launching in your kayak from a ledge above a river by sliding down the bank and dropping into the water.

31. **Sieve:** A strainer created by rocks. Usually very dangerous and should be avoided.

32. **Sluice:** A narrow, tight channel in a rapid.

33. **Spray Skirt:** Made of neoprene, a skirt keeps the water out of your kayak. It fits around the waist of the paddler and attaches to the cockpit lip.

34. **Squirt Boat:** Extremely low-volume kayak allows the paddler to use the underwater river currents for playing.

35. **Strainer:** Extremely dangerous obstacles that clog the current with tree branches or other debris, but still allow the water to flow through. This can trap paddlers and gear and make rescue very difficult.

36. **(to) Swim:** bailing out of an overturned kayak by pulling your spray skirt and pushing yourself out of the boat. Not a decision to be taken lightly, requires you to make a conscious decision to exit your boat. Things to take into consideration: when was your last breath, are you in a pool or in the runout of a rapid. Right in the middle of a big rapid is a very bad place to swim. In the middle of a committing gorge, swimming is not an option. Most importantly, if you swim, you need to drink a beer out of your bootie to ensure your river karma stays positive (provided by Dan Menten).

37. **Take-out:** Ending point of a paddling trip, where the boats are finally taken from the water.

38. **Technical:** A description of the character of a rapid that requires skillful maneuvering and boat control because of frequent obstacles. Technical can also describe specific, difficult-to-master paddling techniques.

39. **Throw bag:** A rescue device incorporating a floating rope coiled inside a nylon bag. This bag is to be thrown while holding one rope end to aid a swimmer.

40. **Undercut:** An overhanging rock or ledge with water flowing underneath it. Undercuts pose the threat of trapping paddlers and gear.

41. **Waterfall:** A major vertical drop in a riverbed(typically over six feet in height).

42. **Wave train:** A series of standing waves usually in the main ⸱⸱rrent at the run out of a rapid.

43. **Wave Wheel:** A playboating move where kayakers cartwheel over a wave train.

44. **Wrap:** To wrap your boat around a rock or obstacle. Wraps can occur after a broach. [18]

For playboating moves such as flips, cartwheels, blunts, loops, etc. see also Playboating, Wikipedia.

# Endnotes

1. Dan Menten.
2. Glaccum, Sean. *Idaho Paddler: Whitewater Gems.* page 100, Joe Carberry.
3. 2003, An Otter Press, LLC
4. Glaccum, Sean. *Idaho Paddler: Whitewater Gems.* page 8.
5. Dan Menten.
6. Dan Menten.
7. Wikipedia. "1999 Salt Lake City tornado." http://en.wikipedia.org/wiki/1999_Salt_Lake_City_tornado. Downloaded 2/12/2010.
8. "Altitude record drop."Freestylekayak.com. http://www2.rocsport.com/cgi-bin/show.pl?action. Downloaded 7/1/2004.
9. "Puerto Viejo de Sarapiqui, Costa Rica. http://www.anywherecostarica.com/destinations/sarapiqui-costa-rica. Downloaded 5/3/2010.
10. "Costa Rica National Parks: Guayabo National Monument." http://www.costarica-nationalparks.com/guayabonationalmonument.html. Downloaded 11/5/2010.
11. Wikipedia. "The Fer-de-lance---Costa Rica's Most Feared Snake." http://sabalolodge.com/blog/2009/09. Downloaded 12/13/2010.
12. Summitpost.org. "Cerro Chirripo." http://www.summitpost.org/printable.php. Downloaded 11/5/2010.
13. *Oregon Kayaking* and <u>Ashland Mine Productions</u>. "Salmon River Canyon." Ben Stookesberry. http://www.oregonkakyaking.net/rivers/salmn_nop/salmon_nop.thml. Downloaded 2/10/2011.
14. *Rapid Magazine.* Spring 2004. "Creekin' Stein River." David Norell.
15. *Lunch Video Magazine* (LVM) #10 Penstock Productions, LLC.
16. *Pulse.* DVD. Tao Films, LLC.. Tao Berman, edited by Eric Link. 2008.
17. "The Comet". 2003. CD and song. Carl Zoolkoski and Phyllis Bengry.
18. Wetdawg.com. "Whitewater Terminology." http://www.wetdog.com/pages/white_tip_display.php. Downloaded 11/5/2010.